27.50

D0906853

SPATIAL ECONOMIC BEHAVIOUR

SPATIAL ECONOMIC BEHAVIOUR

The Microeconomic Foundations of Urban and Transport Economics

R. W. Vickerman

Senior Lecturer in Economics
The University of Kent at Canterbury

St. Martin's Press   New York

Library of Congress Cataloging in Publication Data

Vickerman, Roger William.
  Spatial economic behavior.

  Includes bibliographies and index
  1. Regional economics.   2. Space in economics.

I. Title.

HT391.V52   1980   330   79–25872
ISBN 0–312–75022–6

To Chris

Contents

Preface

The main aim of this book is to provide an introduction to the microeconomic foundations of those aspects of economic activity which have a spatial dimension, the economics of regions, urban areas and transport. There are many good books on the economic problems associated with each of these topics and increasingly they have included reference to recent developments in both the theory and modelling of them. However, there has been little attempt to try and draw together the main strands into an integrated body of theory on 'spatial economics'. In particular there has been a failure to integrate the work on the structure of spatial economies with that on transport.

This book represents an attempt to provide an introduction to some of the literature in these various areas and to make it accessible to students at an undergraduate level as well as outlining the structure of a more integrated approach. There is a rich research literature on aspects of transport and travel choice, location, theories of search and general equilibrium models of land-use and spatial structure which is difficult to use as teaching material both because it is addressed to the profession and because it lacks a framework of reference. At the graduate level the book should provide a suitable introduction to further work on both transport and urban economics courses. The only assumptions made are that students have taken a basic microeconomics course – some revision of the main concepts required is given in Chapter 2 – and have a level of mathematical ability commensurate with that. No more than a basic knowledge of calculus is necessary. Whilst the book is designed for use as an introductory text on courses in urban and regional economics or transport economics, I hope it will interest other students of urban, regional and transport problems and introduce to them the value of economics in helping to understand these. I also hope that other economists may find some interest in this as an application of economic principles.

I am very grateful to successive groups of students taking my courses in Urban and Regional Economics at the Universities of Hull and Kent for their forbearance whilst I was working out the ideas in this book;

they have taught me a great deal. Numerous people have helped me in the production of this final version by commenting on various ideas at earlier stages of development and reading earlier drafts of chapters. I owe considerable debts to my colleagues at Kent and particularly to Ian Gordon, who has helped me crystallise my ideas and shown exemplary patience when I devoted time to this book instead of to our joint research project. John Craven read the final manuscript and rescued me from a number of errors. The final product is nevertheless my responsibility alone.

My greatest debt is to my wife Chris, who once again has not only suffered from my absences during the writing but has laboured on many an evening turning manuscript into coherent typescript and only rarely complained of the constraints placed on her spatial behaviour.

ROGER VICKERMAN

The University of Kent
Canterbury

1 Introduction

One of the curious paradoxes of the modern, developed, capitalist economy is that whilst its very foundation depends on trade, which itself implies the transport of both goods and people over space, many of its most urgent economic problems also concern space. By space is meant the separation of economic activities by distance and the organisation of the economy into distinct areas such as towns and regions. As economies have become richer the variations in the well-being of their residents between such areas have become more pronounced. As transport and communications have improved so the relative lack of mobility experienced by certain groups within the economy has become more pronounced. The easily identified problems of backward regions, decaying urban centres and stagnating public transport systems are not unique to the developed economies; similar problems, often intensified, are also found in many developing countries of the Third World.

Although problems concerning the spatial structure of economies are so dominant economists have been reluctant to incorporate these spatial aspects into a coherent theory of spatial economics. It is true that questions of the spatial organisation of markets had received detailed attention in the inter-war period with the classic analysis of Hotelling (1929) and there is a strong German tradition in location theory, stemming from Weber (Friedrich, 1929) at the beginning of the century, but actually traceable back to von Thünen (Hall, 1966) as early as 1826. However, these partial analyses of specific aspects of spatial economics remained essentially peripheral to the mainstream. The tremendous growth of interest in regional economics and transport economics in the post-war period, and more recently in urban economics as a recognisable separate branch of the discipline, has curiously not led to a significant reversal of this philosophy. Regional economics has concentrated largely on the application of Keynesian and post-Keynesian theories to multi-regional models in which space is ignored. Urban economics has involved essentially a branch of applied welfare economics concerned mainly with those social problems which are characteristically urban, such as housing, pollution, public goods and similar

1

problems. Transport economists have also been rather narrow in their approach. The main economic issues have been those of modal choice and consequent concern with the valuation of travel time and its implications for investment appraisal and optimal pricing, particularly where congestion exists. Rather less concern has been given by economists to the more general questions of accessibility and choice in a spatial economy.

There has, however, been a growing awareness of the limitations of traditional approaches. To some extent this is a reflection of increasing concern with new and rather different problems, the replacement of the traditional transport problems of congested roads and declining public transport with a new concern for mobility as the spatial structure of local economies has changed; the growing awareness that the transport sector (the key feature of any spatial economy) cannot be expanded at will in an age of increasing energy prices; the recognition that cumulative decline can set in not just in regions with structural employment problems but even in the heart of major cities; the growing financial problems of the great cities all over the world. The main thrust of these new concerns is in a recognition that the various strands of spatial economies cannot be considered independently of each other. Greater integration of transport and location questions with the various other concerns of economists, consumption and production in general, requires a consistent and coherent theoretical framework, one which treats the spatial element as an integral part of the decision-making processes of both consumers and producers.

In this book we shall consider the development of such a basic framework as an introduction to the various branches of economics concerned with spatial problems. The emphasis is on the development of a consistent theoretical methodology and the derivation of a modelling philosophy as the basis for empirical work. The book is not concerned with the specific problems of particular forms of transport or particular cities or regions nor is it concerned with the detailed development of policies for use in particular situations, it is based on the belief that only by a thorough understanding of the basic principles can such specific problems and policies be adequately formulated and understood.

There are four stages of development of the analysis. In Chapters 2 and 3 we shall be concerned with the simple analysis of choices and decisions in a spatial environment under various assumptions of behaviour. Chapter 2 takes as its starting-point a basic theory of choice as the cornerstone of microeconomics. This enables us to review the main principles of choice, the roles of preferences and constraints, and also to discuss the possibilities of revising the traditional theories based on the simple choice between goods to consider theories which attempt to decompose goods into various more basic characteristics or to aggregate them into composite activities. Chapter 3 builds on these theories to develop some simple models of the various dimensions of spatial choice, aspects of the travel decisions, mode, destination, frequency of travel, and a theory of location. These various theories which form the basis of much contemporary work on spatial economic problems are seen to be inadequate both in terms of the basic principles of Chapter 2 and in terms of the requirements of a more comprehensive spatial economic model. Out of the discussion emerges the critical importance of the concept of accessibility and the various difficulties associated with both its definition and use. Because of the importance of valuation in so many uses of this type of model there is a short discussion of the derivation of economic values from choice models in an Appendix to Chapter 3.

It becomes increasingly clear during the course of Chapters 2 and 3 that there are basic inadequacies in the traditional partial approaches to these problems. Chapters 4 and 5 tackle the problems of moving from a theory based on the assumption of independent decision-makers with perfect knowledge working in perfectly functioning market situations to conditions more representative of the real environment. Chapter 4 considers the independent decision-maker in an imperfect world of risk and uncertainty. Various modifications to the simple theories can be made to account for various types of uncertainty in which decision-makers are seen to be choosing between various strategies. However, this still supposes that it is possible for the individual decision-maker to determine an optimal strategy from the information available. In the final section of this chapter the concept of search is introduced, where individuals are unaware of the precise nature of the various outcomes and the risks attached to them and hence have to determine a strategy to search for information on these facts and also determine when to stop searching. The importance of this consideration in theories of spatial choice is easily seen. Chapter 5 seeks to relax the independence assumption and consider the effects of conflict between the various agents in the economy. This involves not just the conflict between rival uses of given limited resources but also the strategies involved by decision-makers aware of the effects of their actions on others and the repercussions of others' reactions on them. Once we recognise conflict we also need to recognise the possibilities and implications of co-operation between agents as a means of increasing decision-making certainty. The introduction of collusion also leads us to consider the role of government in the spatial economy in general terms and the possibility of substituting social for individual choices and preferences. We can therefore by the end of Chapter 5 make some revisions to the provisional means of valuing certain characteristics of the spatial economy to allow for social considerations.

We cannot, however, obtain a full and complete picture of the working of a spatial economy without some attempt at piecing the various sectors of the economy together. Chapters 6 and 7 examine the structure of general equilibrium in a spatial economy but then proceed to a critical evaluation firstly of the general equilibrium methodology and then of the relevance of the concept of equilibrium itself in the spatial economy. Chapter 6 is largely concerned with the structure of general equilibrium models, the way they treat the various sectors of the economy and the behaviour of these in equilibrium. Chapter 7 considers firstly an alternative approach using linear programming techniques but then questions the relevance of concepts of overall optimisation. An alternative approach using adaptive rather than full optimising behaviour is outlined. In the third section the possibilities of cumulative imbalance in the spatial economy are considered by reference to some more aggregate models of multi-regional economies.

The various modifications made to the basic model in Chapters 4 to 7 take us a long way from the simple structures of Chapter 3 which form the basis of most practical and policy-related work in this area. Chapter 8 is devoted to an attempt to pull together the various strands into more complete but still operational models which can help us both to understand the structure of local economies and assist in the formulation of policy towards transport improvements and other aspects of urban change. The description of an operational complete model of the urban system which can fulfil both of these functions is still some way into the future but the aim here is simpler: to produce models which capture the essential features of linkage and interaction which prevail in the spatial economy and yet remain workable. With the background of the material covered in the remainder of this book, the economist wishing to tackle the challenging problems of transport, cities and regions should be better equipped to understand the complex linkages and interrelationships which make up any local economy.

A NOTE ON FURTHER READING

This is a short book given the size of its task and can, therefore, only be introductory to many topics whilst on many others only the main threads of the analysis can be outlined. Despite the relative newness of the subject as presented here an enormous literature has developed on specific aspects of the material covered. Whilst it is important to be able to develop certain themes in more detail it has not been thought necessary to attempt an all-inclusive bibliography of every aspect of the subject but rather to pick out some primary references which illustrate the development of thought, provide necessary foundations for the analysis or develop certain points in much greater detail. These are indicated by names and dates in brackets in the text and listed at the end of each chapter. Also at the end of each chapter is a short guide to further reading which serves to collect the more important references together into a more structured form.

REFERENCES

Friedrich, C. J. (1929), *Alfred Weber's Theory of the Location of Industries* (Chicago: Chicago U.P.).
Hall, P. G. (1966), *Von Thünen's Isolated State* (Oxford: Pergamon Press).
Hotelling, H. (1929), 'Stability in competition', *Economic Journal*, 39, 41–57.

2 The Basis of Choice and Preference

The cornerstone of all microeconomics, indeed of all questions with an economic content, is choice. To many economists the rigorous development of a theory of choice has been seen as less important than the important results concerning resource allocation which can be derived from it. Possibly this has been because of the need for practical application of the results of theoretical exercises, but the hiding of an explicit choice theory behind the concepts of utility and indifference has often served to confuse and hinder the acceptance and application of the tools of economics to many problems. Yet ultimately economics is not about as abstract an idea as resource allocation, it is about choice, choice of the individual as to what to do, where to go, what to buy, choice of the producer as to what and where to produce and how, choice of the community how to live and so on.

People, individually or collectively, make choices every hour of every day. Most of these choices (if not all) imply, either directly or indirectly, some form of movement through the space which separates individuals or collections of individuals in an economy. Individuals travel to various destinations about their business and pleasure, the manufacture of goods involves the coming together in one place of materials and labour from many different locations, international business rests on the transmission of messages and money around the world. These are the direct and identifiable incidences of movement, but there are indirect implications too. The use of any good at home carries with it the implication of a shopping trip. Taking this a stage further, the choice of location for a residence, a factory, an office, is itself a sort of capitalisation of future movements. An individual choosing a house does so on the basis of its convenience to his or her workplace, the provision of schools, shops, golf courses, pleasant walks, the view and so forth as well as the house's characteristics. The price which the market determines will reflect a measure of the assessment of all these features by that part of the community directly concerned. Once taken,

6

the location decision fixes the constraints on all future mobility choices by defining the set of choices both necessary and available to satisfy future needs. Similarly we can analyse industrial location in terms of the classic transport inputs approach so comprehensively developed by Isard (1956).

We can see from this general overview of a choice situation that there are several levels of choice involved in a spatial economy which we can reduce to three broad types of decision:

(i) location decisions, taken on the basis of potential future mobility and constraining all subsequent mobility choices in the short run;

(ii) consumption decisions, taken within the constraints set by location, involving all economic activity by the agent in question (consumer or producer) and implying movement through space directly or indirectly as a result of the decision;

(iii) travel decisions, taken within the constraints set by location and the decision to undertake a particular consumption pattern, involving the specific where, how, when decisions relating to mobility.

Whilst this is presented as a hierarchy of choices, the choices are not separate, there is a recursiveness such that each order of choice is conditioned by the subsequent orders of choice implied by it. It could further be argued that in many cases such decisions are taken simultaneously and we shall need to examine what difference such an assumption would make.

Whichever way we choose to look at the problem, however, it will be apparent that some means of representing the cost occasioned by the spatial separation of economic activity and measuring the costs of location in terms of an activity pattern is necessary. This is covered by the rather imprecise term, accessibility, which can mean many different things. A major issue in the remainder of this book will be the recurring theme of how to measure and how to value those concepts included under the umbrella of accessibility.

This is the framework of choices to be analysed, but let us start at the very beginning with a more abstract look at how individual economic agents take decisions. There are two relevant questions to be answered at this stage, what is the set of choices available to a given agent and what is the decision rule by which he selects from the set.

CHOICE AND DECISION

The set of choices in existence at any time is virtually boundless, the typical economic agent could not conceive of all the possible alternatives, and neither could we hope to formalise his choices and model them. For this reason we need to define a sub-set of the set of all choices which we call the attainable set. In the strict language of choice theories, only when the attainable set is coincident with the whole set are choices said to be unconstrained, but it is easy to see that there will be various gradations of an attainable set. Constraints will, in particular, vary with the time-period in question. An individual can easily perceive as an attainable set all the jobs for which he is qualified within an area for which he has knowledge, but he will normally be constrained by a contract of employment to attend his existing job today and for any period up to a month or longer. For the purposes of this book we shall refer to constraints on choice as existing when the *immediately* attainable set does not coincide with the *potentially* attainable set. Potential choices, in this instance, include all those perceived as being attainable within a given time-period longer than the current decision period. We might also note that it may be possible that the potentially attainable set is smaller than the immediately attainable set because of imperfect perception by the agent, but for the moment let us assume that knowledge is perfect, as is customary in the initial stages of development of a microeconomic theory.

Typically the boundary to an attainable set is fixed by the resources of the chooser and the vector of prices attached to the available choices. We must be careful, however, in our specification of resources and prices in a spatial environment since the overcoming of space also involves an outlay of time. This necessitates the specification of a unique price vector for each location which includes the full or, as it is usually referred to, generalised cost of the choice. Similarly, the chooser's budget constraint must include a relevant time-budget. In the limit the time-budget is the natural one, but for many choices the realistic time-budget for the individual is one reduced by a large commitment of time to essential sleep, eating and hygiene activities, and also by working time. For the producer, the time-budget may be less rigid because of variable working practices, shift-work and so forth, and it is more likely that time factors will be explicitly valued in financial costs.

Having thus defined the set of attainable choices and the constraints on choice we need to examine the nature of the decision rules by which the individual can select from the set. It is immediately clear that the set of choices available will be greater than the possible sub-set which can be selected in the typical choice situation and that the individual economic agent is therefore forced to exhibit some preference for one choice to the exclusion of another. In other words there is, implicit in any decision rule, a concept of ordering such that taking any pair of choices from the attainable set the individual can establish an unambiguous relationship between them. If the set of attainable choices is $X = \{x_1, x_2, \ldots \ldots x_n\}$ then the individual can take any pair x_i and $x_j (i \neq j)$ and compare them such that $x_i R x_j$, where the notation of a relationship R means that x_i is regarded as being at least as desirable as x_j. This weak ordering implied by the relationship R is desirable as the basis of a series of axioms of choice behaviour which can be used to derive a pattern of choice decisions exactly equivalent to that implied by the more traditional assumption of the existence of a utility function for the individual.

We do not need to develop and discuss the axiom system and its implications in detail, but let us recall the main properties.

Axiom 1 – Completeness: for any two choices x_i and x_j there exists R such that either $x_i R x_j$ or $x_j R x_i$ or both hold;

Axiom 2 – Transitivity: for any three choices x_i, x_j, x_k, R is transitive such that if $x_i R x_j$ and $x_j R x_k$ then $x_i R x_k$ must hold;

Axiom 3 – Greed: if the choices x_i and x_j are quantifiable in terms of units such as in the classic consumer choice problem where they are vectors representing alternative bundles of the same set of goods, and $x_i \geq x_j$, then $x_i R x_j$ and not $x_j R x_i$ must hold;

Axiom 4 – Continuity: bundles which are numerically close in the sense defined by *Axiom 3* are also close in the sense of ordering;

Axiom 5 – Convexity: if for any three bundles $x_j R x_i$ and $x_k R x_i$ then for any scalar λ, $0 \leq \lambda \leq 1$, $[\lambda x_j + (1 - \lambda)x_k] R x_i$ must hold.

It can easily be seen that the relationship R allows us complete generality although for most cases of choice we shall need to distinguish between the relations of *indifference*, $x_i I x_j$, and *preference*, $x_i P x_j$.

Axioms 1 and *2* can be used to lead us towards a definition of rationality since these are the key assumptions relating to a weak ordering. In addition to being able to state preference or indifference between series of pairs of choices, rationality also implies that the individual has some ultimate goal determining his choice, that is that the choice made is the best in the sense of maximising some objective, profit, utility or whatever. We should, of course, add that this in no way implies that an individual needs to maximise an objectively measurable entity; all we need to say is that *if* an individual can (*a*) weakly order choices and (*b*) assign some *personal* 'value' to the order, he behaves as if he were maximising an entity such as that implied by the notion of utility. The emphasis here is on the uniqueness of the value scale to the chooser such that no inter-personal comparison is possible. It may appear that if we were to model a producer's choice situation then this caveat is unnecessary because we can characterise the objective as a profit function which has some objective value. However, there is no reason why any two producers should have either the same personal valuation of a given financial profit or even that the financial value of the profit is perceived as the whole of the objective function. There is, therefore, no difference in principle between any class of economic agent.

The value of defining an objective function which is to be maximised is in the mathematical convenience of the construct. What needs to be shown, therefore, is the consistency of such an approach with the axiom system outlined. The simplest axiom system used to define rationality will not lead to the existence of a utility function, but the addition of *Axiom 4*, Continuity in Preferences, both ensures the existence of a utility function and its continuity. Without the continuity axiom there could be wide jumps in the ordering, with the possibility of a sudden switch from a choice regarded as worse than a given choice x_i to a choice regarded as better whilst moving along a given sequence of 'bundles' defined by a ray through the origin, without going through a choice which is regarded as indifferent to x_i (as in Figure 2.1).

It is easy to demonstrate that given the first four axioms there exist indifference curves which are continuous and downward-sloping to the right. *Axiom 5* ensures that they are also convex to the origin. It is useful to introduce a sixth axiom at this point, which ensures that such curves are not only convex but are additionally smoothly convex by making the marginal rate of substitution between any pair of choices uniquely determined at all points. Once the indifference curve is shown to be smooth the implicit utility function is differentiable such that a concept of marginal utility can be introduced and, moreover, given strict convexity this marginal utility can be shown to be diminishing as quantity increases although there is no *general* relationship between the convexity property and diminishing marginal utility.

Following this argument demonstrates that given an acceptable set of axioms about the way in which an individual orders choices we can first of all represent the attainment of an optimum by examining classes of choice which display indifference and attaining the highest such class

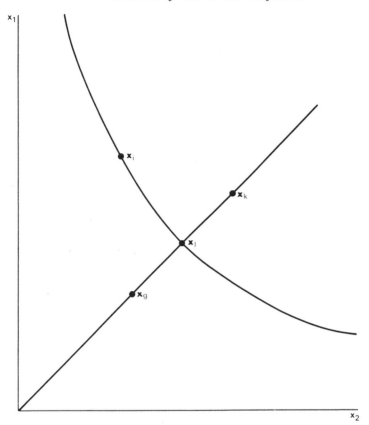

FIG. 2.1 $\mathbf{x}_k$ is clearly preferred to $\mathbf{x}_g$, but between these two there must be an $\mathbf{x}_j$ such that $\mathbf{X}_j I \mathbf{x}_i$.

possible with a given resource constraint. Secondly, it is an easy transition to a representation of this problem as the maximisation of a utility function of this form,

$$U_a = U_a(x_1, \ldots \ldots x_n) \tag{2.1}$$

which is monotonically increasing, continuous and twice differentiable, subject to a resource constraint of the form,

$$\sum_i p_i x_i = M_a \tag{2.2}$$

where the p_i are the prices of the choices x_i and M_a is the resource budget of individual a.

Now if we assume that the economic agent's problem is simply one of allocating all his resources in a given time-period between the attainable set of choices so as to achieve maximum utility we can solve the problem in the sense of producing a solution vector of values of $(x_1 \ldots \ldots x_n)$ which satisfies our aim. Implicit in this solution is the solution vector and the set of prices and the budget constraint,

$$x_i = f_i(p_1 \ldots \ldots p_n, M_a) \tag{2.3}$$

The solution method is the common one of using Lagrangean multipliers to find the maximum value of the function,

$$V = U_a(x_1 \ldots \ldots x_n) + \lambda(M_a - \sum_i p_i x_i) \tag{2.4}$$

Taking partial derivatives of V gives the following set of necessary conditions for a maximum,

$$\frac{\partial V}{\partial x_i} = \frac{\partial U_a}{\partial x_i} - \lambda p_i = 0 \tag{2.5}$$

$$\frac{\partial V}{\partial \lambda} = M_a - \sum_i p_i x_i = 0 \tag{2.6}$$

Interpretation of these conditions reveals that at the solution values which we can call the *optimum* position the ratios of the marginal utilities of two choices will be equal to the ratio of their prices,

$$\frac{\partial U_a/\partial x_i}{\partial U_a/\partial x_j} = \frac{p_i}{p_j} = \text{marginal rate of substitution} \tag{2.7}$$

and λ can be given an interpretation as the marginal response of the utility function to a change in the budget constraint (commonly referred to in neoclassical economic theory as the marginal utility of money). Solution of the conditions for each x_i yields the set of relationships mentioned above as equation (2.3), which is, of course, the set of demand functions for each choice.

We have now shown that an observable and testable set of relationships between choice, prices and resources can be derived from an unobservable utility function which is consistent with a set of axioms concerning behaviour. Furthermore, given the set of demand equations for x_i with the property of homogeneity of degree zero, such that if all p_i and M are changed in the same proportion the x_i remain unchanged, it is also possible to demonstrate the existence of an indifference map of the type implied above. As long as the demand curve is smooth it is possible to demonstrate this principle of *integrability* and hence the existence of an implicit utility function.

Moreover, the implications of *Revealed Preference Theory* are that on a minimum number of axioms the existence of a utility function with the normal properties can also be demonstrated. These axioms are, simply,

(i) in any situation, given a vector of prices and income, the consumer will select a bundle of choices which exhausts the budget;

(ii) choice is consistent in that if a consumer chooses bundle x^o = $(x_1^o, x_2^o, \ldots \ldots x_n^o)$ in one situation of prices and income where x^1 = $(x_1^1, x_2^1, \ldots \ldots x_n^1)$ is also available then he will not choose x^1 in a situation where x^o is still available;

These two axioms together give a rather weak revealed preference system but replacement of (ii) by the stronger axiom,

(iii) given a sequence of bundles $x^o, x^1, \ldots \ldots x^s$, of which at least one is revealed to be preferred to the following one and each and every one is at least identical to or revealed preferred to its successor, then the last, x^s, cannot be revealed preferred to the first, x^o, in any situation where both are available,

enables completion of the necessary transitivity to ensure integrability. The strong axiom ensures integrability and hence the implied existence of the utility function; it is possible to interpret even the weak axiom to this effect.

Finally, in this introduction to choice and preference we need to return to the question of convexity and diminishing marginal utility which, whilst not generally related, were held to be related in certain circumstances. The assumption necessary to achieve this is of independence of the utilities derived from the individual choices. In particular, if the utility function is specified additively,

$$U_a = U_a^1(x_1) + U_a^2(x_2) + \ldots \ldots + U_a^n(x_n) \tag{2.8}$$

then the marginal utility derived from each choice, $\dfrac{\partial U_a^i}{\partial x_i}$, is determined by the quantity of x_i alone, and if this diminishes as x_i increases then the implied indifference curve is convex. The importance of independent utilities, however, is better expressed as implying a situation where the marginal rate of substitution between any two choices in the attainable set is independent of the third. This independence of irrelevant alternatives property will be seen to be of considerable importance subsequently when we consider the separability property of utility functions for practical application.

To summarise this very brief overview of the theory of choice and preference, we have shown that by postulating a simple series of axioms we can derive rules of optimal choice behaviour consistent with a purely mathematical representation in terms of utility functions. Furthermore, this representation is consistent with the nature of demand functions and revealed preference behaviour actually observed in the market-place. However, it is a theory of behaviour based on the premises of perfect knowledge, prior determination of the price vector and resource budget (neither of these being within the individual's control), the absence of risk and uncertainty, and the absence of costs in 'consuming' the choices. All of these issues we shall take up in the following chapter, but first we need to consider more carefully the precise nature of the choices in the attainable set.

DEFINING ATTAINABLE CHOICES

Thus far the analysis has been very abstract in character – we have referred loosely to being able to define a set of alternatives from which the individual economic agent chooses, his ultimate choice being some 'bundle' made up of varying quantities of each available choice. For the purposes of defining the analysis of preferences and optimal solutions this was adequate and had the advantage of complete generality to both consumption and production activities. Now we must be more specific in order to draw out the particular characteristics of choice in a spatial economy.

The production decision is a fairly straightforward one in that the producer, given his interest in a particular market, has to decide between the various mixes of inputs which will give him corresponding outputs. One of the available inputs will be the location, any change in which may affect the delivered prices of both the other inputs and the finished product. We shall return to the solution to this problem presently.

The consumer's decision is a much more difficult one to conceptualise adequately. There are three possible approaches to the question which are worth further consideration, the orthodox goods approach, the household production function approach, and the attributes approach.

The Orthodox Goods Approach

The classic model of consumer choice is concerned with a set of goods, each one being clearly defined and identifiable as different from all others in the set. The consumer's problem is one of selecting bundles of goods and comparing these with each other. Each choice represents a different bundle of the same set of goods. Given the attainable set, X, which consists of a range of such goods, $X = (x_1 \ldots \ldots x_n)$, the consumer can choose a wide range of alternative bundles, e.g.

$$\mathbf{x}^r = \{x_1^r \ldots \ldots x_n^r\}$$
$$\mathbf{x}^s = \{x_1^s \ldots \ldots x_n^s\} \tag{2.9}$$

which can be ranked in the usual way. In the two-dimensional case where the set is of two goods, x_1 and x_2, only the sub-set of bundles which satisfy $\mathbf{x}^r I \mathbf{x}^s$ is the indifference class from which the usual indifference curve between x_1 and x_2 can be drawn up. Any point below the indifference curve, such as $\mathbf{x}^t$ in Figure 2.2, is inferior in the sense that it satisfies both $\mathbf{x}^r P \mathbf{x}^t$ and $\mathbf{x}^s P \mathbf{x}^t$.

The advantage of this approach is that each of the goods is traded, such that an unambiguous price vector is available and the allocation of a financial budget between the goods is a straightforward exercise. The disadvantage, which is critical given our interest here, is that the goods must be identifiable and separate. Furthermore we know that the spatial element in the consumption of ordinary goods is not completely valued by the market. For example, an input of an individual's leisure time or his use of a private car is not included. Finally, many of the activities which our general theory of spatial behaviour must cope with are not traded 'goods' in the sense of normal private goods, they involve externalities and/or varying degree of publicness in being non-rival (one person's consumption does not reduce the quantity available for others) or non-excludable, such that a potential consumer cannot be prevented from consuming by market forces, e.g. by price. This arises essentially when we introduce the time-dimension implicit in space such that goods which are free in the monetary sense now have a price, but a non-market-determined price, attached.

The identifiableness and separableness of goods is of particular importance when we wish to consider quality changes in existing goods or the introduction of completely new goods. Orthodox theory cannot cope with such a situation since it requires a respecification of the choice set, and in an empirical sense does not permit the use of past experience

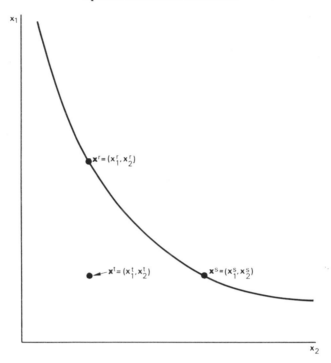

x_1

$\mathbf{x}^r = (x_1^r, x_2^r)$

$\mathbf{x}^t = (x_1^t, x_2^t)$ $\mathbf{x}^s = (x_1^s, x_2^s)$

x_2

FIG. 2.2

to predict future action. Quality change and new 'goods' are likely to be of particular importance in spatial economics because the practical questions to which it is hoped to provide answers are those concerning the siting of new facilities, improvements to transport networks and so forth.

The Household Production Function Approach

The pioneering work of Becker (1965) introduced a valuable new approach of treating consumers as producers. This is specifically tailored to accommodate questions of allocating a time as well as a money budget. Whilst keeping firmly in the sphere of the conventional concept of goods the approach recognises that often utility does not derive directly from individual goods. Many activities involve no consumption of goods at all and many more involve the simultaneous consumption of several goods. What the consumer derives satisfaction from is the activity

$$U_a = U_a(A_1, A_2, \ldots \ldots A_m). \tag{2.10}$$

Each of the activities is produced by the individual by inputs of goods and time,

$$A_k = A_k(x_1, x_2, \ldots \ldots x_n, L_k). \tag{2.11}$$

The level of output is constrained both by overall budget constraints,

$$\sum_i p_i x_i = M \tag{2.12}$$

and

$$\sum_k L_k = L \tag{2.13}$$

If we simplify the problem slightly such that there is only one composite commodity, x, which is used in the production of each activity, it reduces the number of separate variables and constraints. Thus we can rewrite equation (2.11) as

$$A_k = A_k(x, L_k). \tag{2.11'}$$

We can also specify internal consumption constraints which limit the degree of substitution between inputs in the production function (2.11'),

$$L_k \geq a_k x. \tag{2.14}$$

This latter relationship ensures that impossibly small amounts of time are not devoted to certain activities.

Maximising equation (2.10) subject to the constraints of equations (2.11') and (2.12) to (2.14) we obtain the following conditions for an optimum

$$\frac{\partial U}{\partial x} = \lambda p + K_k a_k \tag{2.15}$$

$$\frac{\partial U}{\partial L_k} = \mu - K_k \tag{2.16}$$

$$K_k(L_k - a_k x_k) = 0 \tag{2.17}$$

where λ, μ and K_k are the Lagrangean multipliers corresponding to the three constraints (2.12) to (2.14). A number of points are worth noting here. First of all without the consumption constraint (2.14) we would have the simple results that the marginal rates of substitution between goods equals their price ratios from equation (2.15) and that the marginal rate of substitution between time and goods is given by μ/λ

(assuming $p = 1$ as a numeraire). The effect of the consumption constraint is to modify these two results. Consider equation (2.17) which says that either $K_k = 0$ or $L_k = a_k x$. If the latter is true the consumption constraint is binding and the most interesting effect is on the marginal rate of substitution of time. Since λ is implicitly the marginal utility of relaxing the budget constraint we can divide (2.16) by λ to express in monetary terms and rearrange to give

$$\frac{K_k}{\lambda} = \frac{\mu}{\lambda} - \frac{\partial U}{\partial L_k} \cdot \frac{1}{\lambda} \qquad (2.18)$$

K_k is the marginal utility of relaxing the time consumption constraint and hence equation (2.18) in effect expresses the marginal value of saving time on activity k as the difference between the value of time as a resource (μ/λ) and the marginal value of time in activity k. If, however, constraint (2.14) is not binding $K_k = 0$ and the value of saving time from that activity is zero.

The useful suggestion made by DeSerpa is that activities can be classified according to whether the time consumption constraint is binding. Where it is, individuals value positively savings in time from that activity, otherwise it can be classed as a pure leisure activity in which individuals may positively value the time spent in the activity and not seek savings. Since time is the key feature of the spatial economy it is important that this ambiguity in the way it enters the choice function as both resource and consumption element is clearly understood.

The advantage of the approach is that it can be made all-embracing by including work and other activities as possible choices in the activity set. This effectively makes income a choice variable, within certain constraints, and allows for a trade-off between income and the monetary budget and the amount of leisure time available for non-work activities.

A further advantage is that it is possible to introduce additional constraints into the production relationship to account for the presence of externalities. The demand for individual goods is obtained as a derived demand from the production relationship as for any factor input in a production process. Furthermore, implicit in the allocation of time to activities is a monetary valuation of that time which can be shown not to be just the opportunity cost of forgone work but ultimately a valuation of time savings unique to the activity from which it is saved (DeSerpa, 1971).

The disadvantage is that it still requires us to specify precise activities and precise goods as inputs although to the extent that the means of production of an activity can be varied within the production function we can obtain a qualitative change in the activity. The introduction of a new goods or a new activity requires re-specification of both the production relationship and the utility function. Nevertheless, the principle that an individual chooses between bundles of related goods and time, which can be perceived as complete and independent activities, is an important step towards a more realistic basis for choice in a spatial economy.

The Attributes Approach

Whilst the consumer-as-producer idea gave a new lease of life, and opened new horizons, for the traditional approach it was still clear that there were major drawbacks to these approaches implicit in their basic assumptions. The breakthrough to a new area of consumer theory came simultaneously in both an abstract approach (Lancaster, 1966) and a practical one of considerable relevance to our interests here (Quandt and Baumol, 1966). This approach has come to be primarily associated with its more rigorous foundation in the name of Kelvin Lancaster, and can be generically referred to as the attributes approach.

The fundamental re-think involved in this approach is to ask the question 'what does the consumer consume a particular good or activity for?' The traditional answer is 'to obtain utility' but the revised answer is 'to obtain utility or satisfaction *from certain qualities or attributes* of the good or activity'. This allows us to recognise explicitly that there will often be alternative ways of attaining a given level of utility, not only by trading-off between different bundles of the same goods but by consuming different bundles of different goods which have similar attributes. Furthermore, quality changes of existing goods, or the introduction of completely new goods, can easily be accommodated since, as long as we can specify a finite set of attributes, all goods (current or future) can be assessed in terms of those attributes.

What do we mean by 'attributes'? The conventional economist can specify these for consumer goods in terms of the physical senses or emotional feelings – food has sweetness, texture, etc., clothing has colour, warmth and feel. The spatial economist has, in many respects, a richer series of attributes to consider: all those environmental characteristics regarded as so relevant in many studies of recreation and shopping are attributes, as are the difficult questions of comfort, convenience, etc., which have troubled transport economists. Moreover, it is not only the 'private good' attributes which can be incorporated, we can also deal with externalities such as congestion, pollution, etc., directly since these qualities will appear as arguments of the individual's utility function.

Formally the analysis involves the consideration of three decision spaces – goods, attributes or characteristics and activities. Since it is the attributes which provide the utility we write the objective function,

$$U = U(z_1, z_2, \ldots \ldots z_p). \tag{2.19}$$

Each activity produces a non-negative amount of each attribute such that we can relate each attribute to the level of activity. If this were assumed to be a linear relationship where b_{hk} is the coefficient relating a given level of activity A_k to the appropriate generation of characteristic z_h, then we can write,

$$z_h = \sum_{k=1}^{m} b_{hk} A_k. \tag{2.20}$$

Similarly, since goods go to produce activities, the total amount of each good required for the given level of activity can be expressed, on the same assumption of linearity, as

$$x_i = \sum_{k=1}^{m} a_{ik} A_k. \tag{2.21}$$

The matrices corresponding to the elements a_{ik} and b_{hk} express the consumption technology of the economy. In a simple case there will be a one-for-one relationship between goods and activities such that the latter concept becomes effectively redundant. We would also normally expect the number of attributes, p, to be less than the number of goods, n. We can finally note that the system resolves to the orthodox goods case when $p = n = m$.

The decision problem is then to maximise $U(z_1, \ldots \ldots z_p)$ subject to the consumption technology constraints and the normal budget constraint. With the addition of the usual non-negativity constraints on x_i, A_k, and z_h this becomes a very complex programming problem. Lancaster (1966) has shown that the simplifications introduced in the preceding paragraph can produce a soluble programming format and that many interesting results of consumer choice theory can be derived. Of particular interest are the behaviour and identification of substitute and complement goods, the possibility of zero consumption levels of certain goods, and possibilities of commodity groups and immunity of choice from price changes which are irrelevant in the sense of not disturbing the optimal choice in that sub-set of choices being considered.

Appealing though the attributes theory is, with its ability to produce all the normal behaviour patterns in consumption and to cope with quality change and new goods, can it be turned into a fully operational model? Furthermore, how objective can our definition of attributes be – is it possible to define a completely inclusive set of attributes to cover all cases? In practice the answer to these questions must be no. Yet this does not refute the theory, nor render it an academic *curiosum*. The attributes approach provides a useful organisational model for understanding the process of choice between closely related 'goods' and has been successfully used as a tool of analysis within a number of clearly defined areas. What has not yet proved possible is the building of a general equilibrium system based on this structure. Its value has most clearly been seen in many environmental and spatial situations and accordingly we shall refer to this approach as the logic behind much of the decision-making in this book.

SEPARABILITY

We have so far considered the choice problem as an overall one, the consumer allocating total budgets over all possible choices. In practice, of course, it is rarely feasible to consider such a large task and empirical studies of demand focus on specific sectors or even specific goods or services. This use of an overall conceptual structure on a specific market raises the important question of separability in the utility function.

We used the result previously that if a utility function can be written as additively separable, i.e.

$$U(x_1, \ldots \ldots x_n) = U_1(x_1) + U_2(x_2) + \ldots \ldots + U_n(x_n) \quad (2.22)$$

and each choice displayed diminishing marginal utility then we have both necessary and sufficient conditions for strict convexity in the implied indifference curves. Traditional applications of utility theory used, at least implicitly, this form of utility function as the basis of estimated demand functions and so forth. However, additive separability is an extreme case of separability to which it is not necessary to resort in order to obtain some useful results and guidelines for simplification of the choice system as a basis for empirical work.

The conceptual basis of separability is that the economic agent groups the choices of the attainable set into self-contained sub-sets within each of which he makes allocative decisions, but that decisions taken within one sub-set do not affect decisions taken in other sub-sets.

This is equivalent to arguing that prior to the optimal choice decision governed by the utility function there is a division of expenditure into broad budgets, e.g. housing, fuel, food, travel, recreation. Choices between the groups are formed by a sort of super utility function. Hence, if the choice set is exhaustively separable into s groups, we can write, in general form,

$$U = U[U^1(\mathbf{x}^1), U^2(\mathbf{x}^2), \ldots \ldots U^s(\mathbf{x}^s)] \tag{2.23}$$

where $\mathbf{x}^1$, $\mathbf{x}^2$, etc. represent vectors of choices. In this format the marginal rate of substitution between any two choices in, say, $\mathbf{x}^1$, is independent of any choices in $\mathbf{x}^2, \ldots \ldots \mathbf{x}^s$. This general presentation is known as *weak separability*, since it makes no further demands on the system.

Various stronger forms of separability have been proposed which tighten up the relationships between the choices in the system. Of these the most important is additive separability, which requires the overall utility function to be additive across the individual functions,

$$U = U\left[\sum_{r=1}^{s} U^r(\mathbf{x}^r) \right]. \tag{2.24}$$

This implies the stronger result that the marginal rate of substitution between any two choices in any two groups is independent of any choice in any third group. A possible refinement to this is the use of indifference curves which are homothetic to the origin, leaving the marginal rates of substitution between any two choices constant along all rays through the origin; and hence the elasticity of demand for any choice with respect to total expenditure on its own group is unity. Such homogeneous separability involves separating out all choices which do not display similar income elasticities, that is necessities, luxuries and inferior choices must never appear in the same group.

The relevance of a careful investigation of the possibilities of separability in any application can easily be seen. In effect the utility function, be it one with goods, activities or attributes as arguments, is split into two, one sub-set of choices being variable or alternative-specific, the remainder remaining unchanged by any decisions taken with respect to the variable sub-set: these can be regarded as generic. The inclusion of choices which are really related to the alternative-specific set in the generic set will lead to biased results. Hence in any choice decision enormous care must be taken in understanding the appropriate links between the choices under observation and all other possible choices. We shall see eventually the critical nature of this result in the particular case of multi-level choices.

INTERDEPENDENCE OF DECISIONS

If we return briefly to consider the sort of choices which face us in an analysis of a spatial economy, particularly those of location and travel decisions referred to earlier, we can see clearly the problem which will arise in an attempt to produce a coherent model. The particular difficulty we face is that of the interdependence of decisions in a spatial economy, that interdependence arising out of the spatial dimension. When interdependence is present the separation of choice determinants into alternative specific and generic factors becomes difficult since the number of truly irrelevant alternatives from which choice in a particular situation is fully independent will be very low. Without being able to use the separability property in the chooser's objective function more complex simultaneous decision procedures become necessary. Such a solution is an unfortunate one since it suggests that any realistic modelling of behaviour in a spatial economy will result in an impractically large, and, what is more, potentially insoluble model structure.

What is required, therefore, is some means of simplifying the problems to a manageable size in a rigorous way whilst retaining the basic features of interdependence. Empirically this could be resolved by analysis of variance procedures, given complete information on the whole system, to identify the main interdependencies, but this too is not a practical solution. It may, however, be possible to synthesise the choice structure without needing recourse to information on the *ex post* revelation of preferences.

If we characterise the problem in the framework of decision theory we are recognising that the outcome of any particular decision is influenced to a greater or lesser extent by a wider range of decisions taken both prior to and succeeding the decision in question. For this exercise we assume that the decision-taker is fully aware of all the outcomes of possible decisions and the full range of choices available. Each of these outcomes can be represented by a pay-off, the value of some objective function which it is desired to maximise, such as utility or profit. In the absence of risk, uncertainty or conflict with other decision-takers, as assumed thus far, the decision problem in the state of independent decisions is no problem. The final choice is clear, that decision with the highest pay-off is unambiguously the best selection.

However, if choices are not independent this implies that the pay-off varies according to the decisions exercised elsewhere; the problem now is to maximise the combined pay-off of several decisions, thus implying that the maximum pay-off from any single decision is no longer an unambiguously best choice. The pay-off from each alternative can therefore be expressed as itself a vector of pay-offs, each element representing the pay-off from that alternative, given a particular sequence of related decisions. We thus have an $m \times n$ matrix of pay-offs, p_{ij}, with m rows representing the alternatives available for the decision in question $(x_1, \ldots \ldots x_m)$ and n columns, each representing an alternative structure of related decisions $(y_1, \ldots \ldots y_n)$.

	y_1	y_2	$\cdots\cdots y_j$	$\cdots\cdots y_n$
x_1	p_{11}	$p_{12}\cdots$	$\cdots\cdots p_{1j}\cdots$	$\cdots\cdots p_{1n}$
x_2	p_{21}	$p_{22}\cdots$	$\cdots\cdots p_{2j}\cdots$	$\cdots\cdots p_{2n}$
x_i			p_{ij}	
x_m	p_{m1}	$p_{m2}\cdots$	$\cdots\cdots\cdots\cdots\cdots\cdots$	$\cdots p_{mn}$

Given complete certainty and knowledge of all possible alternatives the decision problem is simply to choose x_i and y_j such that p_{ij} in the above matrix is at a maximum. From the point of view of decision theory this is a trivial problem given that all the states, both x and y, are under the decision-maker's control and that he has perfect knowledge of the relevant p_{ij}. What is more interesting is the structure of the pay-off matrix since this will help us to tie in some of our later discussion with the introspective theories of consumer behaviour used so far.

Note that from this general case we can identify independence and interdependence in decisions and, even more important, the degree of interdependence. If for any x_i, p_{ij} is constant over all j then that choice is independent. This would be an odd case since, in general, if p_{ij} is constant over all j for one x_i we would expect p_{ij} to be constant over all j for each and every x_i. This gives us a clear case of independent decision making since max.(p_i) will give us max.(p_{ij}).

A second case is that of simple interdependence, where choosing y_j such that p_{ij} is a maximum gives the same y_j for all x_i. In the extreme case the ordering of the p_{ij} over j for each i would give the same ranking, but for this simple decision-making case the order of the non-maximum p_{ij} is irrelevant to the decision. This result is interesting because it suggests that where one sequence of decisions dominates the choice, the variation in pay-offs attributable to other, non-dominating, sequences is irrelevant. Remember that we have defined the conditioning states, y_j as sequences of decisions for generality, so the simplification is not just one of identifying a single related decision. Nevertheless, this result does suggest that the possibility of defining dominating sequences of decisions could be a means of achieving considerable simplification. In terms of our utility theory model we are saying that, although there is an apparent relationship between separated sub-groups of choices such that the marginal rates of substitution are not fully independent, in a multi-dimensional choice situation these cases will be interior rather than boundary cases and hence will not affect the ordering of preferences. If this is true we can separate the choices without upsetting the final choice analysis.

The final case is of complex interdependence where the ranking of p_{ij} by j is different for each i such that each possible sequence of decision taking, y_j, which conditions the choice under consideration, x_i, will lead potentially to a different optimal x_i. Even without this problem there may be the possibility of identifying a dominating sub-set of y which will consistently yield higher pay-offs for all x_i than all other y_j and thus enable a partial simplification. The effect of this is to reduce the variance of the pay-offs in the non-selected sub-set to zero or very close to it. It would seem highly unlikely that we should identify many situations in which anything other than a fairly small sub-set of y would dominate and hence the potential simplification would be considerable.

What we have shown, therefore, is that the interrelationships will only matter if they upset the preference orderings. Let us return to our various spatial choices and consider the likelihood of this situation. With travel choices, except in special cases such as work journeys, it is unlikely that choices are separable. With location decisions it is reasonable to expect that one or two activities will dominate the choice, for example work, educational and possibly shopping journeys in the case of residential location. Problems are more likely with consumption choices where it is less clear immediately the extent to which necessary travel inputs will cause individuals to change preference orderings, nevertheless further investigation should reveal the scope for such simplifying processes.

It must be remembered that we have considered the problem of interdependence and separation purely in terms of the preservation of preference orderings. Returning to the pay-off matrix it will be recalled that a dominant strategy y_j was one which consistently yielded the highest p_{ij} for all x_i. Let us also consider the case where, although the p_{ij} alter with the choice of y_j, the choice of y_j does not alter the preference ordering of x_i, i.e. max.(p_{ij}) over all j always yields the same x_i. This will free the choice of x_i from that of y_j but with a variable pay-off, the preference ordering is unchanged and therefore the independence preserved. However, the value of the objective function has been changed and therefore we must recognise that reproducing preference orderings does not necessarily imply a maximisation of an objective function – the economic agent could be at a local maximum in what is obviously a non-smooth function but not at the overall maximum. This point will need to be recalled if the preference structure is used as part of an evaluation exercise, a point we shall take up in Chapter 7.

We have now established the basic tool kit for analysis of spatial economic behaviour, one which does, so far, differ little from that for non-spatial choices except for the remaining problem of being unable to assume away easily interdependence between choices through their spatial content. However, there is still much to be done to produce a framework for realistic analysis of behaviour when it is remembered that so far we have assumed perfect knowledge, certainty and complete freedom of action and choice. In a subsequent chapter we shall take up two important modifications to the analysis to account for risk and uncertainty and the need to search for optimal solutions. In order to do this we shall rely heavily on the decision theory framework.

SUMMARY

The purpose of this chapter has been to review the relevant tools of economic theory which form the basis of any study of consumer or producer behaviour, the individual agents within the economic system. A thorough understanding of the content of the chapter is an essential prerequisite to any subsequent discussion of specific spatial choice situations. The main theme of the chapter is that it is possible to move from fairly simple and straightforward axioms about choice behaviour through an initial model of great complexity to a situation of simple predictive models which have restrictive but, as it turns out, in many circumstances quite acceptable assumptions. The discussion of transport and location choice models in later chapters will depend critically on an assessment of the reasonableness of such assumptions in specific situations.

There are three main issues which have been raised in the course of this chapter. Firstly, we considered the way in which, given a rank ordering of preferences, behaviour can be analysed in an objective way using the mathematically convenient idea of the maximisation of an objective function subject to constraints. This, in particular, leads us to the convenient position of being able to consider just changes and values at the margin in many situations. Secondly, we had to give detailed attention to the nature of the choices over which preferences are expressed, especially with regard to the consumer's choice. In particular, the adequacy of the concept of conventional 'goods' as the medium of choice has been questioned. We recognised that in our spatial economy we are even more aware of individuals producing and consuming more composite entities, often involving several 'goods' as well as other inputs such as that of time. However, whether we should characterise choice behaviour in terms of these more aggregate entities, 'activities', or rather in terms of a smaller range of the 'attributes' or 'characteristics' possessed by conventional goods or activities is an important question. We shall consider and compare these in practice in later chapters.

The final concern of the chapter has been the extent to which we can simplify the choice problem by considering specific choices as independent from all others. We shall argue at several points the interdependence of many choices in a spatial economy such as that between location and transport choice, but we must also consider the choices of the whole range of consumer goods, or all the possible production processes and products which a firm may be capable of using or making, before we can legitimately use these techniques. This question of separability will also occur at several points in subsequent chapters.

GUIDE TO FURTHER READING

The best single source on the basic theory of choice is the book by Green (1976). The topic of separability is covered by Gorman (1959) and Strotz (1957, 1959) and well reviewed in Simmons (1974). For the basis of decision-making see Edwards and Tversky (1967); the relationship between decision theory and economics is discussed by Baumol (1977) and a considerable amount of decision theory in relation to spatial problems by Isard (1975).

The definition of goods in terms of excludability and rivalness is well discussed by Peston (1972). The household production function is due to Becker (1965) and various developments are outlined in Becker (1976). Particularly important modifications to the theory are discussed by DeSerpa (1971, 1973), de Donnea (1972), Evans (1972) and Gronau (1977). Lancaster (1966) outlines the attributes theory but a parallel analysis of transport mode choice in terms of 'abstract modes' is due to Quandt and Baumol (1966). An interesting recent application of the concept to wilderness recreation is included in Cicchetti and Smith (1976).

REFERENCES

Baumol, W. J. (1977), *Economic Theory and Operations Analysis*, 4th ed. (Englewood Cliffs, N.J.: Prentice-Hall).
Becker, G. S. (1965), 'A theory of the allocation of time', *Economic Journal*, 75, 493–517.
Becker, G. S. (1976), *The Economic Approach to Human Behaviour* (Chicago: Chicago U.P.).
Cicchetti, C. J., and Smith, V. K. (1976), *The Costs of Congestion: An Econometric Analysis of Wilderness Recreation* (Cambridge, Mass.: Ballinger).
de Donnea, F. X. (1972), 'Consumer behaviour, transport mode choice and the value of time: some microeconomic models', *Regional and Urban Economics*, 1, 355–82.
DeSerpa, A. C. (1971), 'A theory of the economics of time', *Economic Journal*, 81, 828–46.
DeSerpa, A. C. (1973), 'Microeconomic theory and the valuation of travel time: some clarification', *Regional and Urban Economics*, 2, 401–10.
Edwards, W., and Tversky, A. (eds) (1967), *Decision Making* (Harmondsworth: Penguin).
Evans, A. W. (1972), 'On the theory of the valuation and allocation of time', *Scottish Journal of Political Economy*, 19, 1–18.
Gorman, W. M. (1959), 'Separable utility and aggregation', *Econometrica*, 27, 469–81.

The Basis of Choice and Preference   29

Green, H. A. J. (1976), *Consumer Theory*, rev. ed. (London: Macmillan).

Gronau, R. (1977), 'Leisure, home production and work – the theory of the allocation of time revisited', *Journal of Political Economy*, 85, 1099–123.

Isard, W. (1956), *Location and Space Economy* (Cambridge, Mass.: M.I.T. Press).

Isard, W. (1975), *Introduction to Regional Science* (Englewood Cliffs, N.J.: Prentice-Hall).

Lancaster, K. J. (1966), 'A new approach to consumer theory', *Journal of Political Economy*, 174, 132–57.

Peston, M. (1972), *Public Goods and the Public Sector* (London: Macmillan).

Quandt, R. E., and Baumol, W. J. (1966), 'The demand for abstract modes', *Journal of Regional Science*, 6, 13–26.

Simmons, P. J. (1974), *Choice and Demand* (London: Macmillan).

Strotz, R. (1957), 'The empirical implications of a utility tree', *Econometrica*, 25, 269–80.

Strotz, R. (1959), 'The utility tree: a correction and further appraisal', *Econometrica*, 27, 482–8.

3 Simple Spatial Choice Models

Building on the theoretical background of Chapter 2 we are now in a position to develop some simple models of choice. In so doing we shall in effect be providing a review of many of the models of spatial behaviour which have been used in the past. These models relate to decisions taken in a world of perfect competition and certainty and where there is no cost of acquiring information. Also we are assuming that neither the actions of a decision-maker nor those of any other individual can influence price in any market. These restrictions are obviously unrealistic but are essential if we are to make progress in understanding the working of a spatial economy. In later chapters we shall introduce relaxations of these assumptions to produce greater realism.

THE TRAVEL DECISION

It will be recalled that we have three levels of decision which concern us in the spatial economy, location, consumption and travel. For reasons which will become clear as we proceed it is more satisfactory to consider these in the reverse order even though we know that each lower-order decision is constrained by those at higher levels.

The travel decision is itself a multi-dimensional choice variable. Let us assume, as outlined above, that the individual is located in a given place and has a given need for travel as determined by the activity level; these are the primary constraints on the choice to be made. The individual is then faced by four separate, but interlinked, choices, whether to travel or not (frequency or generation choice), when to travel (timing choice), where to travel (destination choice) and how to travel (mode and/or route choice). We have characterised these in a terminology more appropriate for personal travel decisions but the basic elements remain unchanged for freight transport if we replace the word 'travel' with 'consign'.

In many situations the first two choices, frequency and timing, can also be regarded as given. An obvious example of this is the work journey, where within fairly strict limits in the short run an individual will make a given number of journeys to and from work in a given period and at relatively fixed times. Likewise the destination decision is given in the short run for most people. Similar constraints on short-run choice also exist in the case of freight transport, often in the form of contractual arrangements. However, all of these variables can be changed over a long enough time-period and the introduction of new working arrangements such as flexible working hours increases the relevance of timing decisions so it is important that we do not just consider mode choices.

Mode Choices

Whilst changing work patterns and the greater relevance of non-work travel have led to an increasing need to consider less constrained models of choice, the historical development of travel choice modelling has been very largely concerned with purely the mode choice question; and it is with this that we shall start. In its most basic form the choice of travel mode can be represented as a simple binary choice situation. The individual has a given journey to make at a fixed time to a given destination but has within the attainable set a choice of two modes of transport, say car and bus. Each choice can be characterised by a series of attributes, its cost (c), its speed or the time cost (t), accessibility to and from the mode at each end, often referred to as the excess time (a), and the standard of comfort and general convenience such as the likelihood of obtaining a seat (s). These attributes all enter into an individual's utility function and since it can be assumed that similar individuals will display similar preference patterns for these attributes we must also add the effects of the individual's socio-economic status. Typically for travel choices the main socio-economic indicators are seen to be income (y), occupation and car ownership (v).

On the assumption that the relative utility derived from each choice can be represented as some function of the set of attributes then the probability of choosing one mode relative to that of choosing the other is simply the probability that the utility so derived is greater. Thus for any individual choosing between modes k and m we can write

$$P(k) = \text{Prob } (U_k > U_m) \tag{3.1}$$

where

$$U_k = U(c_k, t_k, a_k, s_k, y, v)$$
$$U_m = U(c_m, t_m, a_m, s_m, y, v) \tag{3.2}$$

We can note two things about the structure of this model which will be of interest in subsequent developments. Firstly, choice depends both on the characteristics of the choices and the characteristics of the chooser. Secondly, only the direct characteristics of the alternatives in question are relevant – any other characteristics of the journey such as its purpose or destination are assumed to be common to all the alternatives here and thus of no influence on the probability of selection. This is an important application of the assumption of separability and one which we shall need to consider in some detail subsequently.

Let us turn briefly to means of turning the statements of equations (3.1) and (3.2) into an empirically estimable model. First of all it is clear that we can only hope to obtain reasonable results for situations where the chooser can be expected to be aware of the characteristics of both chosen and non-chosen modes. There is likely to be a problem where for some reason the chooser is captive to one or the other mode for reasons apart from the characteristics detailed or where the chooser is ignorant of the true characteristics. This latter problem of variations between perceived and actual characteristics is one which has troubled re-searchers in this area for a long time; which is relevant, the time actually taken by mode k or the time which the chooser believes it takes? This is a problem which we can only consider in more detail when we relax the assumptions of certainty and perfect knowledge. Secondly, estimation of a direct utility function of the type shown in equation (3.2) is not a practical proposition since it is only an implicit and not an observable relationship and hence alternative means of formulating the relation-ships must be sought. Most of these have avoided the traditional econometric technique of linear regression analysis in favour of methods which involve combining (3.1) and (3.2) into either direct or indirect estimates of probability as a function of either differences in, or ratios of, the various characteristics.

Some of the earliest studies did use regression analysis in a binary dependent variable form as a means of obtaining direct estimates of $P(k)$. Stopher (1968) used this method in a study of passenger mode choice estimating an equation of the form

$$P_k = a + b_1(c_k - c_m) + b_2(t_k - t_m). \tag{3.3}$$

Bayliss and Edwards (1970) in a study of freight mode choice used a similar method for various binary choice situations estimating the probability of a given choice as a linear function of a range of characteristics of both the consignment in question and of the firm sending the consignment. Both of these studies suggested the importance of costs and times in the choice of mode. In the case of freight the length of haul and the weight of the consignment were fairly consistently among the most important determinants. However, there are some fairly serious statistical problems with the regression approach, in particular the lack of independence in the error terms when the dependent variable can take one of only two values. There is also the question of whether the sum of the parameters, which represent the conditional probabilities of the choice being altered by a given variation in the associated variable, should be constrained to equal unity.

A closely related technique which avoids some of these problems is that of discriminant analysis. This was first used in the transport mode choice context by Warner (1962) but one of the most important early applications was that by Quarmby (1967). Discriminant analysis starts with the same basic information as does the regression approach, a binary dependent variable and the same series of determining independent variables. However, instead of estimating a direct probability function as in (3.3) it attempts to identify a function which can divide or discriminate the total population of choosers into the two sub-populations of those making each choice with the minimum amount of misclassification. The estimated parameters, instead of being conditional probabilities, are thus weights attached to each variable indicating its relative importance in assigning an observation to one choice or the other.

From the discriminant function $D(k)$ where

$$D(k) = a + b_1 (c_k - c_m) + b_2 (t_k - t_m) + b_3 (a_k - a_m) + b_4 y \qquad (3.4)$$

the probability can be estimated since

$$P(k) = \frac{\exp(D(k))}{1 + \exp(D(k))} \qquad \cdot(3.5)$$

where $\exp(D(k))$ is the exponential function $e^{D(k)}$.

There remains a problem with this approach since the normal means of estimating the parameters of (3.4) does not provide normal significance tests for either the parameters or the overall level of fit. These can, however, be inferred from the parallel regression analysis since the parameters estimated by this approach obey a proportionality with those of the discriminant function. The findings of studies such as that of Quarmby, which used discriminant analysis, are qualitatively similar to the earlier studies, once again emphasising the importance of the relative characteristics of the choices over those of the chooser.

Despite the plausible and, at least on the surface, acceptable nature of the results produced by these methods there was basic dissatisfaction with two main aspects of them. Firstly, on statistical grounds there are difficulties with both approaches which are likely to lead to consistent bias and to difficulties in expressing the significance of both individual parameters and the overall fit. Secondly, there are some more fundamental questions of the logic of the models and their ability to handle both multiple choices and related choices in a consistent manner, which we shall see to be important presently. The basic requirement is for a model which enables the direct estimation of a probability of selection with well-defined distributions of errors and parameters and which can handle all varieties of choice situation. These requirements have been seen to be largely met by the development of logit models.

So far we have only presented a very loose derivation of the model in the form of equations (3.1) and (3.2). The introduction of the logit model enables us to consider this in a little more detail. There are in fact two alternative ways of deriving the logit formulation from simple assumptions about choice behaviour. The original formulation, following the work of Luce (1955), uses essentially psychological notions of utility which have come to be termed assumptions of strict utility. Rewriting the equations (3.2) in the form $U_k = (X_k, S); U_m = (X_m, S)$, where the X_k and X_m represent the specific characteristics of the choices and S refers to the socio-economic characteristics of the chooser, then the relative odds of choosing k and m can be written

$$\frac{P(k)}{P(m)} = U_k/U_m \qquad (3.6)$$

If we assume that the choices of k and m are independent of all irrelevant alternatives it can be shown that the ratio of probabilities is completely defined by (3.6). The problem with this approach is, however, in this very restrictive assumption of complete independence when we are already aware of the many interdependences between choices in spatial situations. The effect of the assumption is that the introduction of spurious alternatives, the classic example being buses of a different colour, leads to quite wild changes in the probability of selection.

The alternative approach developed by McFadden (1973) assumes a stochastic element in the utility function such that for a given individual

$$U_k = U'_k(X_k, S) + \varepsilon(X'_k, S) \qquad (3.7)$$

the second element of (3.7) being unique to the individual. Since this element is stochastic this assumption of random utility implies that the X'_k are specific attributes of each choice. Estimation then requires a distributional assumption for the $\varepsilon(X'_k, S)$. Using the Weibull distribution a probability density function can be derived for $P(k)$ from the hypothesis that

$$P(k) = \text{Prob}[U'_k(X_k, S) + \varepsilon(X'_k, S) > U'_m(X_m, S) + \varepsilon(X'_m, S)];$$

$$\text{for all } k \neq m \qquad (3.8)$$

$$\text{from which } P(k) = \frac{\exp[U'(X_k, S)]}{\sum_j \exp[U'(X_j, S)]} \quad \text{for } j = 1 \ldots \ldots n \qquad (3.9)$$

which for the binary case is exactly the same formulation as obtained for the discriminant function in equation (3.5) except that here it is estimated directly. The random utility assumption avoids some of the more severe independence of irrelevant alternative problems by its introduction of the stochastic elements; the final form to be estimated is, however, identical.

The logit model can be estimated directly for both binary and multiple choices so that direct estimates of probabilities of choice can be made where there are three alternatives (car, bus and rail, for example) without having to resort to rather artificial combinations of choices which are necessary in the case of purely binary estimation procedures. Many studies have estimated first a public–private transport split and then re-estimated for the split between bus and rail in the public case. The nature of the variables considered as influences does not differ from earlier models, at least in the simple mode choice model, and similar results in terms of the most significant determinants emerge with time and cost elements dominant.

It was briefly mentioned earlier that there has been some discussion of the correct form of the various relative characteristics used as independent variables. Some studies have argued that the critical factor is not the relative amount of time or cost saved but the absolute amount, since it is this which features in the resource constraints. Others argue that a saving of ten minutes or an outlay of ten pence alters in its significance from a journey of fifteen minutes at a cost of twenty pence to a journey of three hours at a cost of five pounds. Both of these points obviously have a valid basis and indicate clearly both the care which must be taken in formulating a problem according to the specific circumstances, urban or rural or inter-urban travel, work or non-work journey and so forth, and in interpreting and generalising from the results obtained in one set of circumstances. It is of interest to note that much of the development of mode choice modelling has been occasioned rather less by the desire to produce a fully consistent model of spatial behaviour than by the pressure to produce values of time savings for use in appraisal exercises. The detail of the debate on this issue is beyond the scope of this book but it does have some interesting corollaries for the application of behavioural models. Some of the main issues are discussed in the context of estimating values from parameters of the model in the Appendix to this chapter.

Destination Choices

It is clear from the above discussion that there has been no shortage of consideration of the problem of mode choice; that of destination choice has received much less attention. A number of reasons can be advanced for this. The pressure for disaggregate models as a means of improving the accuracy of forecasts concentrated on the mode choice situation because the greater planning concern has been seen as that of congestion caused largely by the excessive use of private vehicles. Also the main gap in evaluation exercises was of accurate values of time; the development of these disaggregate models offered the best opportunity of producing such values. Adequate results for planning purposes could be derived from the application of more traditional aggregate distribution models developed from the gravity model. This was particularly true in so far as the main concern was with the commuting journey for which no short-run choice of destination exists. Increasing concern with journey purposes other than commuting, particularly shopping and recreational journeys, has led to much greater emphasis being placed on the choice of destination. Furthermore it becomes necessary to consider destination and mode choices as being much more interdependent than traditionally assumed, so that a methodologically consistent approach is necessary for both decisions.

The gravity hypothesis is one of the longest-established models of spatial behaviour. It is an aggregate view of spatial relationships developed formally in the 1940s as part of the social physics attempts to apply the methods of the natural sciences to the study of society (Zipf, 1949). However, the basic concept is also found clearly in much earlier models involving space, particularly the location models of von Thünen (Hall, 1966) and Weber (Friedrich, 1929). In its simplest form the gravity hypothesis asserts that the amount of interaction between two locations, whether in the form of travel or any other form of economic activity, will be proportional to the economic size of the two locations and vary inversely with the distance between them. Hence we can write

$$T_{ij} = kM_iM_jd_{ij}^{-\alpha} \tag{3.10}$$

where T_{ij} is the number of trips from i to j, M_i and M_j are the sizes of i and j which could be represented by population, income or some other variable as appropriate, d_{ij} is the distance from i to j, and k and α are constants. Most discussion has centred on the form of the distance deterrence function or more commonly the generalised cost function strongly related to distance. Early studies used a linear distance function ($\alpha = 1$) but this is unrealistic for the same reasoning that lies behind the difficulty over ratio or difference forms of the time and cost variables in the modal choice models. The physical analogy suggests a value of $\alpha = 2$ and this has come to be one of the most widely used imposed values. A number of studies have used various iterative methods to try and obtain an estimate of the best fit value of α, that is the value which fits a model of the form of (3.10) most closely to observed spatial flows. These suggest that values between one and three are the most appropriate, variations taking place according to the nature of the activity or commodity in question. The power function is not totally satisfactory since it tends to lead to a rather too rapid decay in interaction. This may be appropriate in certain cases but in general is not typical. For this reason greater use has been made of exponential and gamma functions such as the logistic which, although also asymptotic, tend not to eliminate interaction at such low levels.

The gravity model has been widely used in the study of all forms of spatial interaction, travel, both passenger and freight, forms of interaction not implying direct physical movement such as telephone calls, flows of funds, and location and migration. The gravity formulation has the advantage that its inverse can be used as a measure of the relative attractiveness of particular locations. If the opportunities available at a particular location are assumed to be proportional to its economic size then the attractiveness of destination j to those individuals at i can be represented as

$$_iA_j = k'M_j.f(d_{ij}) \tag{3.11}$$

The total attractiveness of location i for the activity in question can then be obtained by simple summation of the appropriate $_iA_j$ over j. This term, the potential of location i as it is often called, is thus

$$P_i = \sum_j k' M_j \cdot f(d_{ij}) \tag{3.12}$$

Hence we have, albeit still at an aggregate level, a consistent means of formulating both movement and location decisions. However, it is necessary to consider more carefully the economic basis of the gravity hypothesis since its adoption has frequently been for reasons of its ability to simulate observed patterns rather than its theoretical soundness.

Various attempts have been made to provide an economic justification for the gravity hypothesis in terms of more conventional utility maximisation criteria. Niedercorn and Bechdolt (1969) have offered an explanation of the normal gravity hypothesis starting with an individual utility function dependent on levels of interaction with persons or things at various destinations. The utility function is constrained by the cost of access and the total travel budget. Maximising individual utility subject to the resource constraint produces a series of optimising conditions which yield an expression for an optimal level of interaction or trip-making in terms of the expected variables, the travel budget, the cost of access and the relative probability of interaction at a particular destination, which is assumed proportional to population. Aggregation over all individuals at a particular origin yields an optimal aggregate level of trip-making in a form consistent with the gravity model of equation (3.10). The problems with this form of aggregation are first of all the need to assume identical utility functions for all the individuals concerned and also the structural ones of whether trips themselves are separable decisions entering the utility function directly and that trips are discrete, integer variables and not the continuous variables implied by the analysis.

Wilson (1970) has attempted to provide a more thorough theoretical justification for the spatial interaction model using the concept of entropy, which has better statistical properties. In a later development (Wilson, 1973) he has suggested that instead of trips entering the utility function the more appropriate level of decision-making is that of total transport consumption (expenditure) or total travel (trips to all destinations). Once total levels of activity are determined Wilson argues that distribution of this travel to destinations, etc., can be adequately handled by the entropy-maximising distribution model.

The development of models at this more aggregate level of total trip-making, considering the reaction not just of trips to particular destinations but of the total travel pattern to changes in specific access costs, has been very slow. One approach followed the development of the abstract mode concept by Quandt and Baumol (1966). This involved the estimation of econometric demand models for individual modes on individual links of a network as a function of both modal characteristics and origin and destination characteristics. This produced reasonably satisfactory estimates of demand elasticities and had the advantage that it estimated total trips rather than a probability and hence could meet the need for making trip production a function of trip and destination characteristics. However, a major problem was found to be the non-independence of estimates to irrelevant alternatives. A particular problem was the sensitivity to the number of alternatives offered, even if some of these possessed identical characteristics. An alternative approach used individual rather than aggregate observations and attempted to estimate total trip production as a function of individual characteristics and measures of total attraction and accessibility (Vickerman, 1974a; Robinson and Vickerman, 1976). An interesting development of this would be to link the trip production function with an expenditure function both at the purely transport level and at the transport-using activity level to accord with the structure suggested by Wilson, a development which we shall consider further in Chapter 8.

Within this framework it may be the case that aggregate distribution models of the entropy-maximising type can adequately handle the straightforward prediction of travel flows. However, an internally consistent approach also requires that the choice of destinations be considered at a disaggregate level similar to that for mode choices. This is particularly necessary for the evaluation of changes in behaviour. The logit model of equations (3.7) to (3.9) can easily be transferred to any choice situation with an appropriate redefinition of the characteristics of the choices available. However, it is this definition of destination attributes which has occupied much of the discussion which has taken place on this topic. In particular we need to consider whether it is possible to define such attributes objectively or whether the circular reasoning of aggregate gravity models, where attraction can be determined from the observed flows through a model constrained to produce known total arrivals and departures for each zone i and j, can be applied.

For work journeys of individuals there is little difference between an objective measure in terms of a variable such as job availabilities and the observed level of employment except where vacancy rates differ substantially between areas. Similarly if we consider freight flows it is likely that there is a very close relationship between the attractiveness of a market and the flows already moving to that destination. When we come to consider those spatial flows which are less constrained in the short run, such as the shopping and recreational journeys of individuals mentioned earlier, it is easy to see that greater scope for variation exists, especially to the extent that in many cases the attractiveness of a destination to the individual may be inversely related to its popularity with others although this question of conflict will be left to a later chapter.

For shopping we have a variety of possible measures of attractiveness. Many early studies of shopping behaviour, particularly those which relied on aggregate flow data, used aggregate data on shopping supply such as floorspace. There is, however, a logical problem in introducing a pure supply factor into what is essentially a demand model. Floorspace is, however, a reasonable proxy for the likely range of shopping facilities available at a destination. Some observers have taken the view that shoppers do not perceive aggregate measures of this type but take a more arbitrary and qualitative view of shopping centres, based particularly on the presence of particular shops. This use of key store indicators can not only provide a measure of attractiveness but can also be a useful means of classifying centres into their respective orders in a shopping hierarchy. This approach has its obvious merits for calibrating shopping models but is still heavily dependent on supply-side factors which are not easily predictable into the future; they lack true objectivity, unless a model of the supply side is also included. Other features of shopping centres, such as their environmental quality or availability of car parking facilities, have also been used as determinants of destination choice.

The selection of destination attributes for personal recreational journeys presents an even more complex task. Here a wide range of largely subjective indicators is relevant, covering various environmental aspects or the quality of facilities provided.

Rather more objective criteria can be applied to destination attributes for freight flows since these will obviously be perceived by potential shippers as part of normal market research exercises. Conventional socio-economic indicators of income and social class will be the main influences. However, once again here we see the problem of interdependence being raised, since the value of these indicators will itself depend on location and other decisions taken by those forming the market.

We have seen in this brief review that there exists a wide range of potential attribute measures for destinations for most types of journey purpose. In many cases there is likely to be a problem in defining satisfactory objective indicators which can be understood and perceived accurately by individual decision-makers. Furthermore we have encountered the major logical problem that many of these indicators are themselves the result of spatial economic decisions taken by other groups. Whilst many of these may be distant enough decisions to be regarded as given and exogenous for the particular decision in question it is clear that care must be taken. We shall take up later the more formal consideration of this interdependence of decisions.

So far we have only considered the attractiveness of the destination, but choice of destination cannot be based on this alone since the relative spatial distribution of alternative destinations will clearly be important. There are two possible ways of proceeding. We could simply regard location as an attribute of each destination and accordingly introduce either the pure distance or the generalised cost of reaching that destination from the origin in question. An alternative approach would be to recognise that individuals may trade-off different attributes differently over space. In this case each attribute would require deflating by the appropriate distance or generalised cost function. Whilst this second approach is an interesting one in that it implies rather more clearly that individuals select attributes as the main determinants of utility and are therefore interested in the spatial distribution of attributes, in practice it will normally only be feasible to consider the available bundles of attributes which emerge as separate destinations. We shall therefore proceed under the assumption that there is only a single distance factor for each destination which represents an averaging of the distance functions for the various attributes.

However, even if we assume the same cost of access to each attribute at a destination it is clear that there is not a single unique such cost for each destination for all individuals. Only if we were to measure this cost of access by straight-line distances would this be the case. Once we attempt to allow for the existence of transport networks, even if we measure distance rather than a generalised cost, we see that the spatial distribution of destinations cannot be divorced completely from the availability of transport modes or the choice of mode made by an individual.

Integrated Travel Choices

If mode and destination choices are closely linked in this way so that variations in modal attributes may alter the relative costs of access to different destinations and hence destination choice, we must consider the most appropriate way of relating the decisions in the modelling context. Is it, for example, adequate to estimate an independent mode choice model and then use the results of this to weight the various modal costs in order to produce a composite cost of access allowing for the likely use of each available mode? It has been argued by some writers that the decisions are inseparable – modal factors influence destination choice but simultaneously the attributes of destinations can affect the relative weighting given to a mode of transport.

In a model designed to explain shopping behaviour Richards and Ben-Akiva (1975) have developed a multiple-choice logit model of the type presented in equation (3.9), in which each mode and destination pair is treated as a separate choice. Hence we can write the probability of using mode m to reach destination d as

$$P(m, d) = \frac{\exp[U'(X_m, A_d, S)]}{\sum_j \sum_i \exp[U'(X_j, A_i, S)]} \qquad (3.13)$$

where the characteristics of mode m are given by the vector X_m and of destination d by vector A_d. A range of alternative specifications was tested on data for the Netherlands. Typical mode characteristics related to in-vehicle time, excess or access time, waiting time, and money costs. Destination characteristics were limited to employment in retailing. Personal factors were mainly represented by ownership of cars, mopeds and bicycles. Although the results were not conclusive they did suggest substantial differences, particularly in the weights attached to time characteristics between sequential and simultaneous models, which at least suggests that the structure of the model could lead to important differences in the valuation of certain changes.

However, there are severe problems with this approach. The main one is the rapid multiplication of choices as the number of modes and, more particularly, the number of destinations increase to a realistic number. This difficulty does assume that individuals always consider the whole range of potential destinations. A study of shopping behaviour in Britain has suggested that the number of alternative destinations considered by individuals in the short term is very restricted, possibly no more than five for many people (Robinson and Vickerman, 1976). This restriction is less likely to apply to some other activities such as personal recreational trips but there the rationale for simultaneous choice of mode and destination may be less clear anyway. Apart from the major problem of the number of choices, which leads to computation and estimation difficulties because of the large number of potential choices many of which have very low probabilities of being selected, there may also be problems with the inclusion of a wider range of attributes, some of which are destination ones and some modal. Interpretation of the effects of certain variables may be made more difficult in such a model form.

The alternative approach is to combine the choices in a recursive manner as developed principally by McFadden (Domencich and McFadden, 1975). In a recursive structure the various decisions are factored in a choice hierarchy rather like the traditional aggregate models which had generation, distribution and modal split models. This ordering of the hierarchy is preserved but in a probability framework. Each lower-order probability of choice is viewed as a conditional probability given a certain outcome of the higher-order probability. Since it is a conditional probability we can estimate the probability of a lower-order choice independently of the probability of selection of a particular choice in a higher order. However, the recursive structure means that the higher-order probability can be affected by decisions concerning lower-order choices. In our two stages considered so far of mode choice and destination choice we are arguing that the probability of selection of a given mode of transport is not affected by the probability of selection of destination, once that destination is known. However, the probability of deciding on one destination will be affected by factors relating to the mode choice decisions. The final compound probability of choice of destination and mode can then be obtained in the usual way. In summary we are saying that the probability of choosing mode m, given destination d, can be estimated from the straightforward logit model as a function of relative modal attributes as detailed previously;

$$P(m|d) = f(X_m, X_k, S) \qquad (3.14)$$

The probability of selecting d is determined by its attributes, A_d, but also by the attributes of the various modes of transport serving it:

$$P(d) = g(A_d, A_i, f'(X_m) \cdot P(m|d), f'(X_k) \cdot P(k|d), S) \qquad (3.15)$$

from which the overall probability of choosing m, $P(m)$ is given by

$$P(m) = P(m|d) \cdot P(d) \qquad (3.16)$$

The power of the recursive model is in its ability to deal with much larger numbers of possible alternatives in total because of the factoring into a series of separately estimated choice functions. In many cases it may be possible to retain binary choice form with a consequent saving in computation. Furthermore, each choice is primarily a function of the attributes of that choice and its alternatives, the effect of lower-order choices is captured in a single variable, termed the inclusive price, which we must now consider in greater detail since it forms an essential part of the argument of the rest of this chapter.

The inclusive price of an alternative is the perceived cost of that alternative to the individual taking into account all the costs which will be incurred in its selection and, where there are alternative methods of achieving that selection the costs of each separate way are themselves weighted by the probability that that means of achieving it is selected. Thus in our destination choice example, in choosing between alternative destinations the chooser wishes to know the total cost of reaching each destination. Each destination can be reached by more than one mode of transport, the relative characteristics of the modes not necessarily being constant for all destinations and hence their probabilities of selection varying. The relevant inclusive price must therefore take into account those characteristics, their weightings relative to each other for that mode and destination and the probability of selection of each mode. More formally, estimation of the basic logit model of equation (3.9) yields a set of coefficients β relating to the attributes of the modes such as times and costs. These β measure the relative weighting given to each attribute in the mode choice exercise. The inclusive price for travel by a given mode m is obtained by applying these weights to the actual attribute values for that mode such that

$$\hat{p}_m = -(\beta^t t_m + \beta^c c_m) \tag{3.17}$$

in a case where there are just the two attributes time and cost, and in general for more attributes

$$\hat{p}_m = -\sum_j \beta^j X_{jm} \tag{3.18}$$

These inclusive prices can be estimated for each available mode k (k $= 1 \ldots \ldots m$) and then the probability of choosing destination d in preference to i can be written as

$$P(d) = g(A_d, A_i, \sum_k P(k) \cdot \hat{p}_k, S) \tag{3.19}$$

Equation (3.19) has a rather convenient form for the economist since it expresses the probability of selection (demand) as a function of the attributes of the choice, the socio-economic characteristics of the chooser which determine preference patterns, and price. It therefore can be regarded as a demand function, albeit a probabilistic rather than a quantitative one. This approach thus enables us to render spatial choice situations in a form which is much more familiar than at first appears likely from earlier models of spatial behaviour. Not only is the form familiar, it is also simple since a complex range of factors is reduced into a single variable representing all the relevant cost-of-access factors. Furthermore this is not an arbitrary selection of a proxy variable as used in many earlier models with rather limited success (Vickerman, 1974b) but a perceived price estimated from the observed behaviour of individuals.

It can also be noted that the price variable behaves like any price. If travel times or costs to a particular destination are reduced then so is the inclusive price of that destination and hence we should expect an increase in the probability of its selection. If there is a universal improvement in the performance of one mode then not only does the use made of that mode increase but also the probability of potential travellers choosing destinations where that mode has a comparative advantage over others. It could also be suggested that if the inclusive price of one destination appears too low then its probability of selection will increase, but through such effects as congestion its inclusive price of access will rise relative to other destinations and there is therefore a sort of equilibrating mechanism to allocate potential traffic between alternative destinations not only on the basis of their own attributes but also on the basis of characteristics of the transport links concerned. Price is determined thus by the interaction of supply and demand. We shall have to leave the question of equilibrium and the detailed mechanism of price changes until a later chapter since it requires the use of certain concepts which we have not yet discussed.

We have spent a considerable time building up a basic model of choice for just two aspects, mode and destination choice, of one of our original dimensions of spatial choice, travel. Now we have established a basic model we can proceed rather faster since it becomes clear that this basic model is applicable to a wider range of choice situations than we have so far considered. The remaining aspects of the travel choice, such as timing and frequency of journeys, can be handled by a simple extension of the model outlined above to additional levels of choice. Timing of journeys could be argued to be either a higher level of choice than that of destination or a lower level: the decision taken on this matter will affect whether it is inserted in the model after or before destination choice. Frequency is more easily classified as a higher level of choice such that destination characteristics affect it in a recursive manner. With these higher levels of choice the basic procedure outlined in equations (3.17) to (3.19) is followed. An inclusive price of the lower-order choices is estimated and this is used, together with their respective probabilities of selection, as a determinant of the alternative selected at the higher level of choice. Thus we can see that the inclusive price used as a determinant of frequency of travel for a particular purpose reflects the attributes of the various destinations available, variations in characteristics between different times of the day and the characteristics of the main modes of transport available. Changes in any one of these various characteristics will alter the inclusive price and hence the probability of undertaking a journey for a particular purpose at a certain frequency. This presents an endogenous way of deriving the basic variables for use in total trip generation so that all levels of travel choice are treated in an internally consistent manner. This approach has the advantage of providing a single modelling structure for use in all types of travel situation whichever level of choice is considered the most appropriate for separate examination.

THE ACTIVITY DECISION

Our next task is to relate the frequency of travel decision to decisions concerning the activity, whether this is a consumption or a production decision. Our final model of the previous section enables us to estimate a probability of travel frequency, given that an activity is to be undertaken, in the light of the various facets of the spatial economy and its transport network. The typical transport model, whether of passenger or freight movement, ignores this in effect by assuming that either the activity level is given or is subsumed into the socio-economic variables. On the other hand conventional, non-spatial models of economic activity concentrate on the explanation of levels of activity per period regardless of how or where they are undertaken. Both of these are clearly inadequate for a complete understanding of the spatial economy.

Two simple examples should suffice to illustrate the problems here, one from production and one from consumption. Production studies are primarily concerned with levels of output and techniques of production which can be somewhat crudely represented either as maximising output subject to a production relationship and a given level of costs or as minimising costs of production subject to the technical conditions and an output constraint. Freight transport studies concern themselves with moving given outputs between points of production and markets. Obviously there is an important link through location but we are not yet ready to consider this, so we shall assume that all locations are fixed for the decision-period in question. There is still a very important spatial link into the production decision which is more easily seen if we consider production as a genuine flow process through time, as suggested by Alchian (1959), rather than as a series of discrete decisions relating to discrete time-periods.

The critical link between production decisions and the various transport decisions we have considered so far is in terms of stock levels. Since the distribution of goods and services takes time the efficiency of the distribution network will be critical in deciding on production plans. We shall need to develop this point a little more fully in the context of investment decisions but that is best left for a discussion of location later in the chapter.

A similar problem occurs in the case of consumer shopping behaviour. Conventional studies of demand or household expenditure aim to explain total levels of purchase per period but no consideration is given to the method of goods acquisition. For our purposes there are two matters of interest, the method of purchase and the frequency and structure of shopping activity. Not all acquisitions of goods imply shopping travel by the purchaser, often the cost of acquisition is borne at least partly by the seller through free delivery or subsidised packing and postage costs or in the case of mail order through catalogue costs and discounts to agents; all of these alternatives are of interest in the spatial economy. The frequency and structure of shopping journeys are influenced by many factors. The growth of car ownership makes shopping on a large scale much easier, journeys for several purposes can be combined without difficulty. The widespread use of freezers reduces the necessary frequency of shopping even for convenience goods. The growth of large out-of-town shopping complexes, either of the shopping mall type so characteristic of North America or of the hypermarket type most actively pioneered in France, encourages the making of longer but less frequent shopping journeys. Hence it can easily be seen that there is a large area of ignorance at one of the most critical links in the spatial economy, that point where basic demands are turned into potential spatial interactions.

The need is therefore clear – to move away from the traditional divisions which regard the demand pattern as one set of decisions and the travel pattern as another set which simply takes the demand pattern as given and implicitly assumes a fixed relationship between the one and the other. Possibly only in the area of recreational and tourist activity has any serious recognition been given to this problem, because of the rather different attitude to travel which may be expected here. The majority of models still regard travel for most non-recreational purposes as purely a disutility, a regrettable facet of life which must be minimised. Better understanding of the role which travel decisions play in activity decisions could well change this view. Before we can develop a model to cope with this additional problem we must examine the location decision since this too is involved in any attempt to produce a more integrated model of behaviour in a spatial economy. An outline of such a model is presented in Chapter 8.

THE LOCATION DECISION

The decision on location either of residence for the consumer or of plants for the producer is the highest-order decision. It represents both the decision which, for most individuals, is the least easily changed in the short run and the one which, when taken, provides the most binding constraints on the remaining choices in the spatial economy. It should also be clear from the earlier parts of this chapter that it would be wrong to examine the location decision independently of the organisation of the rest of the economy, the chosen activity pattern and the provision and characteristics of the transport networks. Hence whilst the location is assumed given, and hence the spatial structure of the economy is treated as fixed, these serve as determinants of both activity and travel choices; but when the opportunity to take a location decision arises the critical determinants are likely to be the desired activity pattern and the attributes of the associated travel.

Basic Location Models

This obvious dependence of location both on other activities and on transport has been a feature of location models since the very earliest. Von Thünen's early attempts to describe the spatial structure of the economy depended on the definition of market areas to describe the hinterlands of particular locations (Hall, 1966). Whilst von Thünen's main concern was to identify order and hierarchies in the economy the critical role of distance in defining market areas and the fact that optimal sizes of such areas would differ with commodities (it was essentially an agricultural theory) and hence with the likely transport costs is identified.

Von Thünen's theory sets out to explain the organisation of agricultural activity. Assume that all activity takes place on a featureless plain consisting of land of equal quality (these are only simplifying assumptions to avoid too great a complexity of variables). The rent that any producer will be prepared to pay for a given unit of land, $\hat{r}_i$, will be determined by its output, q (assumed constant), the price per unit at the market, p (again assumed constant by virtue of the assumption of a single market where perfect competition between producers obtains), direct costs of production c (constant for the same reasons as output and price), the transport rate per unit of distance, t (constant by virtue of perfect competition or no discrimination between users in the transport sector) and distance from the market, d_i, i.e.

$$\hat{r}_i = q(p - c) - qtd_i \qquad (3.20)$$

This maximum rent, later called the bid-rent by Alonso (1960), is determined uniquely by the location of the site. Thus far we have assumed a single activity. If we introduce a second activity it is obvious that q, p and c will not be constant and also it is likely that t will vary according to weight or any special carriage requirements of the product. However, since perfect competition and freedom of entry prevails we would not expect the profitability at the most favoured location, where we can assume t to be arbitrarily close to zero, to differ since if it did all producers would change production with consequent changes in price to restore an equality of profit. Hence the only change to be made if we have more than one activity is to introduce t, the transport rate, as a determinant of r_i. It is then obvious that by knowing the transport rates for commodities we can derive the locational pattern of production about the market. High-transport-cost activities will locate at a close distance and low-transport-cost activities will take locations further away. We can derive a relationship between r and d for each t, the maximum r_i payable at each d_i will determine the activity which will locate there. Following Alonso this is most easily represented as a series of bid-rent curves as in Figure 3.1.

Von Thünen's approach is very simple and abstract and does depend critically on the existence of perfect competition but it has dominated thinking on location since, precisely because of its simplicity and because of its predictive ability. However, we need to develop certain points a little further to deal with the rather greater complexities of industrial

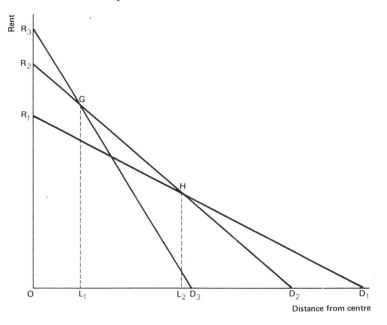

FIG. 3.1 Lines R_iD_i are defined by equation (3.20). Points L_1 and L_2 define important switchpoints in land use between activities with different bid-rents. The line R_3GHD_1 is the revealed rent function for the area on the basis that land is allocated to the highest bidder.

location. When we consider industries other than agriculture it is clear that simple assumptions about locational indifference as far as costs of production are concerned are inapplicable. The main developments in this direction came again in the German tradition in economics, being primarily associated with the work of Alfred Weber (Friedrich, 1929).

Weber also started with the basic premise that particular locations do not have cost advantages in the actual manufacture of goods. However, in addition to land most manufacturing industry requires inputs of more than one factor of production and unlike land these other factors cannot be assumed to be uniformly distributed in general. The location of a plant will therefore depend on the relative pulls of the various material locations and the market; Weber assumes these to be points rather than areas for simplicity. Assuming that for a particular product these various points are not coincident the critical factors to be considered will be the relative weights of inputs and outputs and the distances over which these must be moved, since transport rates depend on these two factors. The main interest was whether industries would locate nearer to the market or to the source of materials and this could be related, through the transport costs, to whether the production process was weight-losing or weight-gaining. The materials index, the ratio of material weights to product weight, is a crude measure; but it suggests that high values would involve a location dominated by sources of materials and low values (less than unity) would involve market domination, whilst values of about one would suggest locational indifference. The basic locational criterion is thus one of minimising total transport costs, assuming that market price of the product and prices of factor inputs are given, and independent of location the optimal location involves finding a set of d_f and d_m to minimise T where

$$T = tw_1 d_{f1} + tw_2 d_{f2} + \ldots \ldots + tw_n d_{fn} + td_m \qquad (3.21)$$

t being transport costs per ton-mile, $w_1 \ldots \ldots w_n$ are the weights of inputs required per unit output, the d_{fi} are the distances each input must be moved and d_m refers to the distance to the market. Obviously the d_{fi} and d_m are not independent and, given the values of t and the w_i, setting the value of any one distance will determine all the others. This is not easy to represent simply algebraically, and typically for exposition a physical analogue is used to represent the situation displayed in Figure 3.2.

The most interesting result which emerges from this type of model is the dominance of end-points – for many processes one 'corner' appears dominant and indifference or trade-off solutions are of little importance. This is confirmed by the refinements to the Weber model developed by Isard (1956). Isard used Weber's basic philosophy but placed it back more firmly in the context of neoclassical economics, using the concepts of substitution and transformation. The transport occasioned by location at a particular site is an input to the production process just as much as raw material or labour. Producers face a range of feasible sites, each of which has a given transport input requirement in terms of ton-miles of carriage at known freight rates. Assume that the requirements of other inputs are given for a known level of output, then the problem becomes one of trading off the various transport requirements to minimise total transport outlays in a manner analogous to the usual isoquant and isocost analysis of production. Whilst Isard's analysis represents an important formulation of the Weberian philosophy it does not go much beyond Weber's basic ideas. One of the points which does arise from the substitution idea is whether transport can be traded off against other inputs in such a way that firms not only choose optimum

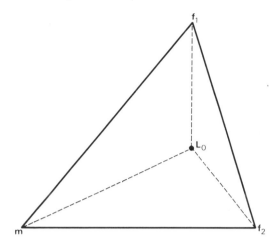

FIG. 3.2 Locational triangle relating the market, m, to the two factor inputs, f_1 and f_2. The distances mf_1, mf_2 and f_1f_2 are geographical distances between the points. The optimal location for a plant, L_0, depends on the effective forces represented by the lines linking it to each corner, these forces being proportional to the relative weights of inputs or outputs as taken into account in the Materials Index. L_0 can also be found by constructing circles representing isocost lines centred on each corner of the triangle and examining their intersections.

sites on the basis of minimising total transport costs for a given combination of inputs and outputs but can substitute a transport-intensive technique of production for one intensive in another input. Although this point did receive attention in an early attempt to improve on Weber's basic model by Predöhl (1928), such an approach has not generally been used. Whilst we do not have the space to develop such a model here it can be seen to be potentially of some importance in cases where firms relocate in the hope of finding a cheaper source of one input, such as labour or land typically, and consequently increase the necessary transport inputs to their operations.

The logical culmination of this approach is found in the work of Lösch (1954). Lösch's work represents a logical extension of the Weberian philosophy to include the influence of demand and potential market areas on location and hence to discuss rather wider questions of the spatial organisation of the economy. To some extent discussion of the Lösch model takes us ahead of our current concern towards a general equilibrium model of the spatial economy, but it is worth while to make some brief comments on the basic model here. In some respects

Lösch committed a disservice to the development of spatial economics. His model was claimed to be a considerable advance on that of Weber by moving to a world with demand and a world of areas rather than points. However, the replacement of Weber's point sources and markets with Lösch's uniform areas is not an obvious move forward. The conclusion that optimal market areas are regular hexagons is not a surprising one from the assumptions used. In addition Lösch's remarks about the relevance of empirical testing, fitting his model to the real world, which he regards as less important than internal consistency and reason, were not the most tactful. What Lösch failed to make sufficiently clear and what is often ignored in assessments of the Löschian model is that in contrast to Weber's concern with the behaviour of locators Lösch's concern is with ideals, with optimal spatial arrangements. This difficult dichotomy between the model designed to explain, predict and evaluate changes and the model designed to seek the ideal is one to which we shall return in Chapters 6 and 7.

Whilst the spatial structure of agriculture about towns and the location of industries received a considerable amount of attention both in a theoretical context as outlined above and in applications of the basic von Thünen and Weber models to empirical evidence the internal structure of urban areas and intra-urban location questions only received detailed attention at a much later date. As with the original von Thünen model, concern with intra-urban location focused more on the results of that location on urban rent structures and land-use patterns than with individual location decisions. There has also been much greater emphasis on residential location than on industrial location although the service structure of local economies has received some detailed attention.

Residential Location Models

The main characteristic of residential location models is the form of utility function which is used. Individuals are assumed to have demands for particular sites because of the characteristics of the site itself and the nature of its location. The primary requirement of location is normally taken to be access to the place of work. The simplest form of the model is the constant expenditure model used by Wingo (1961). This makes the assumption that a household locating in a less accessible (more distant) location will require compensation in the form of lower costs at that location, and assuming that there are no spatial variations in other prices rents at this location must be lower. If they were too low people would wish to gain by moving to that location, thus bidding up rents until the rent differential exactly offsets the extra travel costs. Thus we can write

$$r_i s_i + t_i = \overline{E} = t_b \tag{3.22}$$

where r_i, s_i, t_i are the rent per unit area, average size of site and transport costs to the city centre (where all employment is assumed to be) at location i, and t_b is the transport costs at the city boundary where it is assumed rents for urban functions fall to zero (i.e. are equal only to the opportunity costs for agricultural use).

A more satisfactory approach avoiding the restrictive assumption of the constant expenditure model is that of Alonso (1964). This model still uses the basic trade-off idea between location rent and transport but within the framework of a utility function. The consumer is assumed to wish to maximise U where

$$U = U(X, s, d) \tag{3.23}$$

subject to a budget constraint given by

$$Y \geq pX + r_i s_i + t_i d_i \tag{3.24}$$

r, s and t are as in the previous model, d is the distance from the central area as a measure of location, X is the quantity of a composite consumption good representing other activities engaged in by the consumer and p represents the price of this good. It is from this model that the bid-rent function for each individual can be derived as the maximum amount he is willing to pay for a site at a particular location, which would leave him just as well off as at another location, say where $d = 0$.

If we interpret the value of r_i in the above model as being the bid-rent for that location then from the maximisation exercise we derive

$$\frac{dr}{dd} = \frac{p}{s} \cdot \frac{U_d}{U_X} - \frac{1}{s} \cdot \frac{d(td)}{dd} \tag{3.25}$$

where U_d and U_X are the appropriate marginal utilities of location and the composite consumption good. Rearranging (3.25) in terms of marginal rates of substitution we obtain

$$\frac{U_d}{U_X} = \frac{1}{p} \left[s \cdot \frac{dr}{dd} + \frac{d(td)}{dd} \right] \tag{3.26}$$

This result is the basis of an enormous literature, to which we shall return in a later chapter when we need to consider wider general equilibrium issues. It states simply that the incremental satisfaction from relocation (in terms of movement outwards) which is obtained by substituting travel for goods must be exactly equal to the costs of that relocation in terms of changing rent costs and changing travel costs. For simplicity we can assume that the good X is a numeraire with a price of unity such that $1/p = 1$. Furthermore, since the marginal rate of substitution is assumed to be conventionally negative and since transport costs will increase with distance the land costs term must be negative. Obviously sites must always have a non-negative size and hence $\dfrac{dr}{dd} < 0$; we thus have the basic result that rents must decline with distance and hence the normal assumed shape of the bid-rent curve of Figure 3.3.

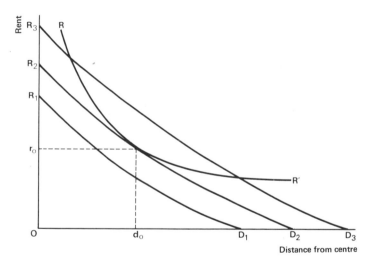

FIG. 3.3 The lines $R_i D_i$ represent a series of bid-rent curves for a given household, the higher the curve the lower the level of satisfaction. The curve RR' is the equilibrium rent function for the city formed as an envelope curve to the various bid-rent lines of Figure 3.1. $r_o d_o$ represents the equilibrium rent and location for this household.

Whilst there have been many improvements and refinements to this basic model of household location, the essential features of a conventional constrained maximisation exercise for a utility function in which location is represented simply with reference to a work journey within what has come to be known as the monocentric city have largely remained. Among the more important contributions are those of Muth (1969), whose utility function concentrates more on housing rather than the somewhat abstract unit of space, and Evans (1973), who linked the utility function to a time-constraint recognising the evidence from transport models that individuals are constrained at least as much by the time-dimension of space as by its cost-dimension. The characteristic feature of most of these models has been their ability to produce the downwards-sloping-to-the-right rent function since all the bid-rent curves are thus shaped.

Muth's model is an interesting alternative to Alonso's since it attempts to combine aspects of housing with land to determine consumers' location of residence. Housing consumption is expressed in terms of units of standard housing – the service provided by the standard house, which is determined arbitrarily but to which all other houses can be related by those variations in price not determined by different locations. A consumer of given income Y at location d_1 has a disposable income of $Y - t(d_1)$ where $t(d_1)$ is the commuting cost from d_1 which can be spent on housing and all other goods and services. The amount spent on housing will be determined by the implicit utility function such that the marginal rate of substitution between housing and goods equals their price ratio in the usual way, as can be demonstrated by the combination h_1, g_1 in Figure 3.4. A location further from the centre at d_2 would involve a reduction in disposable income to $Y - t(d_2)$ necessarily reducing consumer utility unless prices can be changed from $B_2 B_2'$ to $B_2 B_2''$. This is precisely the same process of bidding-up housing prices in less distant areas and forcing down prices in more distant areas to ensure locational equilibrium already met in the Alonso model. Note also that at d_2 consumers purchase a larger quantity of housing relative to other goods than at d_1.

A critical feature of Muth's model is that transport costs depend on income and that the marginal cost of commuting decreases with distance (i.e. commuting costs increase at a decreasing rate). There is some empirical support for these assumptions based on such features as car-ownership levels and the structure of transport rates. A stable equilibrium depends on the marginal saving on housing costs at a particular point for a given level of housing consumption, h, to be equal to the marginal increment in commuting costs,

i.e. $$-hp_d = t'(d) \qquad (3.27)$$

but also that marginal household savings are falling at a faster rate than

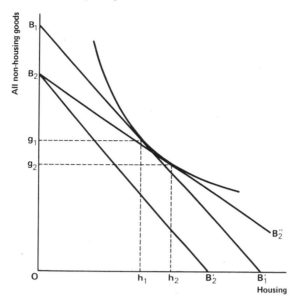

FIG. 3.4 Budget line B_1B_1' relates to net disposable income after commuting costs at location d_1. B_2B_2' and B_2B_2'' relate to net disposable income at location d_2.

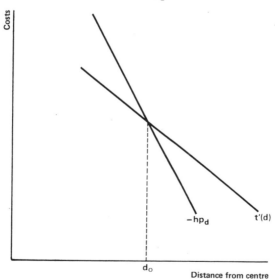

FIG. 3.5

marginal commuting costs as shown in Figure 3.5. If the slopes of the functions in Figure 3.5 were reversed consumers would tend to move away from d_1 since housing savings exceed incremental commuting costs.

The interesting feature of the Muth model is that it ascribes an important role to income, and particularly to the relative income-elasticities of housing and commuting. Muth asserts that the former is greater than the latter, hence for an increase in income from Y_1 to Y_2 the quantity of housing increases from h_1 to h_2 whilst commuting expenditures increase from $t_1(d)$ to $t_2(d)$. The result is depicted in Figure 3.6 as a move in equilibrium location from d_1 to d_2. Whilst the model does not

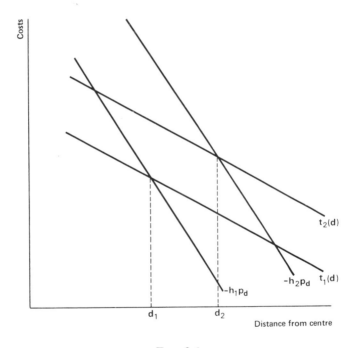

FIG. 3.6

produce a conclusion any different from the Alonso model it highlights the important point that stability in location does depend critically on parameter values, the rates of change of expenditures with respect to income and to distance for a constant income.

A number of writers have questioned the validity of such models in the face of empirical evidence. This had led to rather less simple models based on rather less simple assumptions. The critical features of these more complex models of location is the relaxation of the assumption of a city of individuals with identical preferences such that the effect of different incomes and different income distributions can be assessed. However, introduction of such features takes us rather beyond the scope of our simple choice models and requires us to consider a number of other aspects first.

One thing which will have been obvious from the discussion of location models is that the measurement of location or accessibility in them all is both crude and arbitrary. Certainly it is clear that, in the main, transport decisions have been considered completely separately from location decisions and the evidence of travel-choice models little used as the basis of location choice, with the exception of models such as that of Evans (1973). Furthermore, both of these seem to bear little relationship to the development of models of activity choice. Complexity is an obvious defence. We have already seen how problems multiply as the range of choice-dimensions increases. We have also seen, however, the way in which decisions can be nested and it is but a simple step forward to use the inclusive price concept to build up a means of establishing genuine accessibility prices for locations for individuals or groups of individuals. Such a step would certainly destroy the simplicity of most models of local economies but it might produce both a more realistic structure and a better planning tool.

We have concentrated in this chapter on reviewing the structure of simple choice models within the structure of the choice theories outlined in Chapter 2. We have seen many of the limitations of these models, both in the way they have been applied on a rather piecemeal basis and in the restrictiveness of the assumptions used. The next stage is to introduce some complications to deal with some more realistic problems. There remains the important question of evaluation on the basis of such models, which is covered in the Appendix to this chapter.

Appendix
Valuation in Spatial Choice

Our concern in this chapter has been with models which aim at understanding and explaining observed spatial choices. Many of the models considered, and many more which use similar basic frameworks, are concerned with this objective only as a necessary step in an evaluation exercise. Investment decisions in the public sector and public approval of developments in the private sector have frequently depended critically on the values attached to intangible elements such as time savings, noise pollution, environmental improvement. Useful though pressing policy needs have been in focusing research effort into particular areas, the conceptual and practical problems of producing reliable values are somewhat different from those met so far. Concentration of effort on the refinement of values may have inhibited the development of the wider choice framework. Since valuation techniques have been widely discussed elsewhere it has not been thought necessary to devote a great deal of discussion to this issue here but it is worth while noting the relevant points of contact with the models outlined in this chapter.

Valuation models have typically started with basic choice models of the type discussed above, with optimising individuals making decisions with reference to an overall objective function and in possession of full information. The traditional economic model dealing with choices which are fully priced by a market process provides an endogenous valuation by the usual equating of marginal rates of substitution with price ratios. In this way relative price reflects relative value. This technique cannot be directly followed when either the choice itself does not have a market price, because it is not traded, or is an activity composed of some traded and priced inputs and some intangibles. The spatial choices considered here fall into either or both of these categories.

Two basic philosophies of valuation have been used, the quasi-market-trading approach and the willingness-to-pay approach; we shall consider these in turn, relating them to the basic models developed above. The trading approach is based on the idea that even without markets existing to price them intangibles are traded off by decision-makers, particularly against items which are market-priced. Hence by observing the rate of trade-off an implicit price can be derived which can be interpreted under certain assumptions as a value. This approach has been widely used in both transport and housing choices. The trade-off between cost and time inputs to travel choices can be used to estimate a value of time-savings. House prices can also be seen to be affected by locational and environmental factors such that if sufficient characteristics can be held constant any remaining variations in price can be seen to represent a capitalised value of the varying factor.

We have a choice function of the form

$$G(X) = a + b_1 t + b_2 c \tag{3.A1}$$

where c represents a monetary factor, such as cost, and t a non-monetary factor, such as time, and the values of a, b_1 and b_2 are estimated by one of the procedures discussed in the chapter. The values of these coefficients represent weights assigned by the appropriate statistical technique (regression, discriminant or logit analysis) which estimate the conditional effect of each right-hand-side variable on the choice function $G(X)$. Thus $b_1 = \partial G/\partial t$ and $b_2 = \partial G/\partial c$ and consequently the ratio of these weights is an estimate of rate of trade-off between those factors since, for a constant G,

$$\frac{b_1}{b_2} = \frac{\partial c}{\partial t} \tag{3.A2}$$

Since we referred to the factors here as costs and times, equation (3.A2) gives an implicit rate of exchange of time for money which could be interpreted as a value of time-savings.

How does this value of time-savings relate to the implicit theoretical value discussed in Chapter 2, defined in equation (2.18)? There are a number of difficulties here. First of all we noted there that the value of time-savings depended on both the resource value and its use in a particular activity when the time-constraint was binding. This means that equation (3.A2) is only applicable for active traders of time and money – those who choose an alternative inferior on both characteristics must be excluded. Secondly, what is the role of the constant term in equation (3.A1)? This is frequently included but in practice implies a form of captivity to one or other alternative and hence biases the valuation. If it is not included this implies an equality between average and marginal values of time-saving. Thirdly, we need to consider the role of income. The theoretical model of Chapter 2 made the usual assumption of a constant marginal utility of money such that λ is a constant. Frequently equation (3.A1) has been estimated with an income term on the right-hand side such that any coefficient of this is likely to bias the estimates of b_1 and b_2. Obviously we are interested in the effect of income on choice and on the implicit valuations, but simply introducing income hinders the theoretical justification for interpreting b_1/b_2 as a value. A typical way round this has been to stratify by income such that equation (3.A1) can be estimated for a variety of different groups each with its own value of time-savings.

A more substantial problem with the interpretation of b_1/b_2 as a value of time-savings is in the absence of a perfect market to ensure that at the margin individuals are paying an amount exactly equal to the worth to them of what they gain. The value b_1/b_2 is really more of a *price* than a *value*. Valuation implies not just the price paid but also an assessment of any consumer's surplus over and above that. Various experiments have been carried out to determine willingness to pay, particularly for public goods which are not priced at all. Rather more work of this type has been carried out on housing market problems, particularly to assess compensation values for noise nuisance and benefits of environmental improvements, but recently there has been renewed interest in the concept for time-savings valuation in transport studies and in the assessment of congestion costs in recreation. The great advantage of a willingness-to-pay approach is that it can involve a whole population and not just the observed traders, since it aims to find that amount which will just induce the individual to trade. This amount is deemed to be the consumer's surplus which is currently being derived from the alternative chosen at going prices and is sometimes referred to as a transfer payment since it just induces a change of decision.

In general terms we can say that the value of the unknown item, time, noise, environment, etc., is exactly equal to the known costs borne by the individual plus his transfer payment or surplus. Thus for noise, at the margin, we can say

$$N = D + M + TP \tag{3.A3}$$

where N is the value of noise, D is market depreciation, M is moving costs and TP is the amount which an individual must be offered just to induce him to stay and suffer the noise. In the time-value case discussed before, the relevant value is defined by

$$C + TP = V \tag{3.A4}$$

where C is the cost difference and V is the value of time-savings. TP is here the amount which must be offered just to induce a change of modes on top of the cost-saving, C. These are accounting definitions of values and typically we do not have the appropriate information to measure these. Observations will produce a scatter of points from which an estimate must be made from a physical measure of the unknown effect, e.g.

$$C + TP = \alpha + \beta t \qquad (3.A5)$$

where β is the value of the time-savings and the constant term α is a measure of what may be termed inertia (those other factors not included in the model which still induce the individual not to transfer choices).

All willingness-to-pay approaches do suffer from the need to determine the appropriate transfer payment by questioning intention rather than observing revealed preference and this has been the source of much scepticism about their uses. In particular it is clear that there are (at least) two values corresponding to equivalent and compensating variations in Hicks's definitions of consumer's surplus (Hicks, 1943–44). There is one amount which an individual is prepared to receive to induce him to make a desired decision, switch modes or stay and suffer noise, i.e. to compensate him for lost consumer's surplus. There is another amount which he is prepared to pay to restore himself to his originally preferred situation. Curiously, however, despite the obvious scope for individuals to attempt to influence the decision-making processes of others by inflating their claims for compensation and minimising their offers of such compensation, many studies in various areas of research have managed to produce values which are both credible and consistent.

Valuation is, however, only useful if the incidence of the valued benefits can accurately be assessed. Over-concentration on values of time, values of noise or values of environmental improvement tends to produce simple models of the type of equation (3.A5) and implicit choice functions like equation (3.A1) wherein many important determinants of choice get lost in a catch-all constant term. Overall evaluation of opportunities depends on much wider considerations than just the separate identification and evaluation of the possible effects of individual factors.

GUIDE TO FURTHER READING

There is a vast literature on transport choice, particularly mode choice decisions. Convenient introductions are Hensher (1976a) and Stopher and Meyburg (1975), and a more formal and advanced presentation is in Domencich and McFadden (1975). The development of ideas on passenger mode choice can be traced through Warner (1962), Quarmby (1967), Stopher (1968), de Donnea (1971), McGillivray (1970), Domencich and McFadden (1975), Stopher and Meyburg (1976b), and Hensher and Stopher (1979). Relatively little work has been carried out on freight mode choice but see Bayliss and Edwards (1970) and Watson (1976).

Gravity models date from the social physics pioneered by Stewart (1947) and Zipf (1949). Again a large literature has ensued, most conveniently summarised by Wilson (1970, 1971, 1974).

The relationship with economic models was considered by Niedercorn and Bechdolt (1969) and again, more satisfactorily, by Wilson (1973).

Trip generation has been relatively under-studied. Much reliance has been placed on simple category analysis approaches as of Wootton and Pick (1967) but some attempts at integrating generation into a more systematic framework can be found in Vickerman (1974a, 1974b) and Robinson and Vickerman (1976). Integration of the various stages of choice has only been attempted relatively recently; in addition to the important work of Domencich and McFadden (1975) see also Richards and Ben-Akiva (1975) and Hensher and Dalvi (1978). The direct estimation of travel demand models by econometric means is found in Quandt and Baumol (1966) and some further developments in Quandt (1970). A practical application is found in Domencich and Kraft (1970).

The main developments in location theories can be found in von Thünen (Hall, 1966), Weber (Friedrich, 1929), Isard (1956), and Lösch (1954). Urban location and structure dates back primarily to the work of Park and Burgess (1925) in the 1920s but the main strands in modern thinking are due to Wingo (1961), Alonso (1960, 1964) and Muth (1969). A different approach, which links more closely to the transport models, is that of Evans (1973) and a review of some of the many minor improvements and revisions is contained in Richardson (1977).

The literature on evaluation is vast. The classic foundation of the trade-off approach is that of Beesley (1965) and results are found in many of the studies of travel mode choice starting with Quarmby (1967) and Stopher (1968). An early review is contained in Harrison and Quarmby (1969) and a useful updating in Stopher and Meyburg (1976a). Willingness-to-pay studies of transport include Lee and Dalvi (1969), Wabe (1971) and Hensher (1976b). Other applications of willingness-to-pay approaches can be found in Walters (1975), Starkie and Johnson (1975) and Cicchetti and Smith (1976). More general discussions of environmental evaluation can be found in Whitbread (1978) and Flowerdew and Rodriguez (1978). This list is not intended to be comprehensive, but it provides an illustration of the main approaches used and some of the results obtained.

REFERENCES

Alchian, A. A. (1959), 'Costs and outputs', in M. Abramovitz (ed.), *The Allocation of Economic Resources* (Stanford: Stanford U.P.).

Alonso, W. (1960), 'A theory of the urban land market', *Papers and Proceedings of the Regional Science Association*, 6, 149–57.

Alonso, W. (1964), *Location and Land Use* (Cambridge, Mass.: Harvard U.P.).

Bayliss, B. T., and Edwards, S. L. (1970), *Industrial Demand for Transport* (London: H.M.S.O.).

Beesley, M. E. (1965), 'The value of time spent in travelling: some new evidence', *Economica*, 32, 174–85.

Cicchetti, C. J., and Smith, V. K. (1976), *The Costs of Congestion* (Cambridge, Mass.: Ballinger).

de Donnea, F. X. (1971), *The Determinants of Transport Mode Choice in Dutch Cities* (Rotterdam: Rotterdam U.P.).

Domencich, T. A., and Kraft, G. (1970), *Free Transit* (Lexington, Mass.: D. C. Heath & Co.).

Domencich, T. A., and McFadden, D. (1975), *Urban Travel Demand: A Behavioural Analysis* (Amsterdam: North Holland).

Evans, A. W. (1973), *The Economics of Residential Location* (London: Macmillan).

Flowerdew, A. D. J., and Rodriguez, F. (1978), *Effect of Renewal in Residents' Benefits and Welfare* (London: Centre for Environmental Studies).

Friedrich, C. J. (ed.) (1929), *Alfred Weber's Theory of the Location of Industries* (Chicago: Chicago U.P.).

Hall, P. G. (ed.) (1966), *Von Thünen's Isolated State* (Oxford: Pergamon Press).

Harrison, A. J., and Quarmby, D. A. (1969), *The Value of Time in Transport Planning: A Review*, Round Table 6, Economic Research Centre, European Conference of Ministers of Transport, Paris; reprinted in R. Layard (ed.), *Cost Benefit Analysis* (Harmondsworth: Penguin, 1972).

Hensher, D. A. (ed.) (1976a), *Urban Transport Economics* (Cambridge: C.U.P.).

Hensher, D. A. (1976b), 'Valuation of commuter travel time savings: an alternative procedure', in I. G. Heggie (ed.), *Modal Choice and the Value of Travel Time* (Oxford: Oxford U.P.).

Hensher, D. A., and Dalvi, M. Q. (eds.) (1978), *The Determinants of Travel Choice* (Farnborough: Saxon House).

Hensher, D. A., and Stopher, P. R. (eds.) (1979), *Behavioural Travel Modelling* (London: Croom Helm).

Hicks, J. R. (1943–44), 'The four consumers' surpluses', *Review of Economic Studies*, 11, 31–41.

Isard, W. (1956), *Location and the Space Economy* (Cambridge, Mass.: M.I.T. Press).

Lee, N., and Dalvi, M. Q. (1969), 'Variations in the value of travel time', *Manchester School*, 37, 213–36.

Lösch, A. (1954), *The Economics of Location* (New Haven, Conn.: Yale U.P.).

Luce, R. D. (1959), *Individual Choice Behaviour* (New York: Wiley).

McFadden, D. (1973), 'Conditional logit analysis of qualitative choice behaviour', in P. Zarembka (ed.) *Frontiers in Econometrics* (New York: Academic Press).

McGillivray, R. G. (1970), 'Demand and choice models of mode split', *Journal of Transport Economics and Policy*, 4, 192–207.

Muth, R. F. (1969), *Cities and Housing* (Chicago: Chicago U.P.).

Niedercorn, J. A., and Bechdolt, B. V. (1969), 'An economic derivation of the "gravity law" of spatial interaction', *Journal of Regional Science*, 9, 273–82.

Park, R. E., Burgess, E. W., and McKenzie, R. D. (eds.) (1925), *The City* (Chicago: Chicago U.P.).

Predöhl, A. (1928), 'The theory of location in its relation to general economics', *Journal of Political Economy*, 36, 371–90.

Quandt, R. E. (ed.) (1970), *The Demand for Travel: Theory and Measurement* (Lexington, Mass.: D. C. Heath & Co.).

Quandt, R. E., and Baumol, W. J. (1966), 'The demand for abstract modes', *Journal of Regional Science*, 6, 13–26.

Quarmby, D. A. (1967), 'Choice of travel mode for the journey to work: some findings', *Journal of Transport Economics and Policy*, 1, 273–314.

Richards, M. G., and Ben-Akiva, M. (1975), *A Disaggregate Travel Demand Model* (Farnborough: Saxon House).

Richardson, H. W. (1977), *The New Urban Economics: and Alternatives* (London: Pion).

Robinson, R. V. F., and Vickerman, R. W. (1976), 'The demand for shopping travel: a theoretical and empirical study', *Applied Economics*, 8, 267–81.

Starkie, D. N. M., and Johnson, D. (1975), *The Economic Value of Peace and Quiet* (Farnborough: Saxon House).

Stewart, J. Q. (1947), 'Empirical mathematical rules concerning the distribution and equilibrium of population', *Geographical Review*, 37.

Stopher, P. R. (1968), 'Predicting travel mode choice for the work journey', *Traffic Engineering and Control*, 9, 436–9.

Stopher, P. R., and Meyburg, A. H. (1975), *Urban Transportation Modelling and Planning* (Lexington, Mass.: D. C. Heath & Co.).

Stopher, P. R., and Meyburg, A. H. (1976a), *Transportation Systems Evaluation* (Lexington, Mass.: D. C. Heath & Co.).

Stopher, P. R., and Meyburg, A. H. (eds.) (1976b), *Behavioural Travel Demand Models* (Lexington, Mass.: D. C. Heath & Co.).

Vickerman, R. W. (1974a), 'A demand model for leisure travel', *Environment and Planning A*, 6, 65–77.

Vickerman, R. W. (1974b), 'Accessibility, attraction and potential: a review of some concepts and their use in determining mobility', *Environment and Planning A*, 6, 675–91.

Wabe, J. S. (1971), 'A study of house prices as a means of establishing the value of journey time, the rate of time preference and the valuation of some aspects of environment in the London Metropolitan Region', *Applied Economics*, 3, 247–55.

Walters, A. A. (1975), *Noise and Prices* (Oxford: Oxford U.P.).

Warner, S. L. (1962), *Stochastic Choice of Mode in Urban Travel: A Study in Binary Choice* (Evanston, Ill.: Northwestern U.P.).

Watson, P. L. (1976), *Urban Goods Movement* (Lexington, Mass.: D. C. Heath & Co.).

Whitbread, M. (1978), 'Two experiments to evaluate quality of residential environments', *Urban Studies*, 15, 149–66.

Wilson, A. G. (1970), *Entropy in Urban and Regional Modelling* (London: Pion).

Wilson, A. G. (1971), 'A family of spatial interaction models and associated developments', *Environment and Planning*, 3, 1–32.

Wilson, A. G. (1973), 'Further developments of entropy maximising transport models', *Transportation and Technology*, 1, 183–193.

Wilson, A. G. (1974), *Urban and Regional Models in Geography and Planning* (London: Wiley).

Wingo, L. Jr. (1961), *Transportation and Urban Land* (Washington, D.C.: Resources for the Future).

Wootton, H. J., and Pick, G. W. (1967), 'A model for trips generated by households', *Journal of Transport Economics and Policy*, 1, 137–53.
Zipf, G. K. (1949), *Human Behaviour and the Principle of Least Effort* (Cambridge, Mass.: Addison Wesley).

4 Some Complications: Risk, Uncertainty and Search

Whilst all standard presentations of microeconomic theory and choice behaviour find it desirable to complicate the neat results of choice under riskless, certain conditions by introducing more realistic assumptions of the choice environment, it can easily be seen that consideration of spatial choices requires this fundamentally. The assumption of perfect knowledge specifically falls down when we consider actions taking place over space and whenever there are imperfections in knowledge all actions will be subject to a degree of risk. Risk, however, is a quantifiable phenomenon. The existence of risk implies that although the economic agent does not know precisely the outcome of a given decision he can assign probabilities to those outcomes and hence obtain an expected value. For example, if a businessman is 90 per cent certain of a £1000 pay-off on an action, he can be said to have an expected pay-off of £900 (= £1000 × 0.9). Moreover, he can rank several possible pay-offs and assign probabilities to each, for example, 90 per cent certain of £1000 but with a 5 per cent chance of receiving only £500 and a 5 per cent chance of a zero pay-off: the expected value of the action becomes £925 (= (£1000 × 0.9) + (£500 × 0.05) + (£0 × 0.05)). The essence of risk is that it is quantifiable and therefore that the agent can insure against certain events happening.

However, we also have to recognise that in many cases it is not possible to assign probabilities to an event, even in the Bayesian sense of not knowing exact probabilities but being able to modify prior assignments of probabilities by repeated trials. In this case we are in a situation of uncertainty. Now, there is no clear dividing line between an event with risky and an event with uncertain outcomes. In a sense any decision exercised by an individual in a state of uncertainty implies some subjective assignment of probabilities to the outcome, and hence repeated sampling of the decision by the individual could yield successive modifications to this probability until the individual can assign a probability with a degree of certainty. Many spatial decisions will be of this

69

type–an individual can assign quite reasonable probabilities to the lateness of his bus, or his expected journey time to the office, on the basis of his experience. Less frequently undertaken activities may involve less accurate estimates and therefore be more uncertain but this is only a question of degree. Some decisions will involve a very great degree of uncertainty and, by their nature, repeat sampling is prohibitively expensive – the location decision is one, choices concerning the annual holiday may be another for some people.

Two relevant issues emerge from this: one is the degree of preference for risk or uncertainty an individual may exert, the other is that the cost of a wrong decision may be great and the individual may therefore be prepared to incur some cost in searching for information to improve his knowledge and lessen uncertainty and ultimately the degree of risk.

RISKS AND UNCERTAINTIES

Risk, as we have already seen, involves the economic agent in being able to calculate an expected pay-off or loss from a situation. Let us take a typical spatial choice situation in which, for example, an individual has a clear preference for a particular brand of whisky over all others and his satisfaction (pay-off) from this is independent of where he buys it. Let us also assume for simplicity that this is the only commodity he wishes to purchase. However, his local wine shop, situated five minutes' walk away, does not always stock the brand; on average only seven times out of ten can he purchase it. We can formulate the problem therefore as one of the expected cost of acquiring the whisky as a 0.7 chance of a five-minute walk plus a 0.3 chance of, say, a thirty-minute walk to the next nearest shop, which always has stocks, which produces an expected total round trip of 25 minutes. The question now to be faced is that whilst the consumer displayed a clear preference for his ten-minute walk to obtain whisky over other activities there is no reason why he should prefer an expected twenty-five minute walk over the same set of other activities.

Hence, just as with the usual gambling examples of writers on risk where it is not sufficient simply to compare the gains without reference to the likelihood of achieving them, we cannot in spatial choice expect individuals to rank their preferences for goods or destinations or means of transport or locations independently of the likelihood of achieving the norm level of satisfaction out of the choice in question. Let us take one further example which may help to illustrate the relevance of a norm in a multi-dimensional choice situation, that of the family recreational journey. Assume that the decision-maker has some concept of a minimum level of satisfaction which will just make him undertake a journey in preference to any alternative. The actual level of satisfaction he obtains will depend on the quality of the destination, ability to park, congestion on the journey, freedom from breakdowns, the weather and so on, to each of which we can assume he attaches a probability distribution. If the probabilities are such that his expected satisfaction from each and every choice falls below the norm then he will stay at home.

But this leads us to our first main problem. We have so far compared single risky alternatives with a case of certainty. What happens when every choice has a risk, and more particularly how does an economic agent select between alternatives, as in the case above, which has several attributes each with a probability distribution of risks attached? The solution to this requires our ability to define a function over risk which both reduces all risks to a common medium – typically so that it can be expressed as a monetary gain and loss – and enables us thereby to express preferences over risks.

Preferences over risks, or the probability of an event occurring, can be handled just as preferences over choices. Individuals can express preferences for different forms of risk or different probabilities of events. For example, an individual who prefers choice x_1 to choice x_2 in accordance with the usual rules for choice can be expected to prefer an event with a higher probability of x_1 occurring to an event with a lower probability of it occurring. Thus an individual who prefers rail travel to car can be expected to choose a location where there is a better rail service to most destinations because the probability of there being a convenient rail service for any particular journey is greater. This may seem obvious but has an important implication: what we are effectively doing is combining the probability with the choice pay-off to obtain an expected pay-off or utility from each event. The problem with expected utility is that the compounding of a choice by a probability generates a cardinal measure of utility, not in the sense of an absolute value but in the sense that only certain increasing functions of expected utility which maintain the ratios of utilities will preserve the preference ordering of events.

So far we have assumed that, just as an individual prefers more to less in a state of certainty, he prefers greater certainty to less so that the unambiguous ordering of expected utilities is obtained. We must recognise that there are risk-averters and risk-lovers. Some agents are more concerned with the risk of loss than the expected value of the pay-off such that an event may be chosen simply for its relative certainty.

Although our individual choosing his location prefers rail his concern for the risk of rail strikes, albeit these have a very low likelihood, makes him reject the good rail location for the greater certainty of a car-based location. (In reality these might not be mutually exclusive, of course.) Within the decision framework of the previous chapter we can formalise this pessimistic type of behaviour, and we shall return to this when we consider conflicts with other economic agents in Chapter 5.

Given a pay-off matrix of the type used in Chapter 1 we can interpret the y_j as conditioning events which occur with a known probability for any action x_i. Hence if we have a simple case as in Table 4.1 below where the pay-offs are as given to x_1 and x_2 for each state of y_1 and y_2 but it is known that y_1 occurs with a probability of 0.7 and y_2 with a probability of 0.3.

TABLE 4.1

	y_1	y_2
x_1	100	0
x_2	50	50

Taking strict expected values and the known probabilities the expected value of x_1 is 70, that of x_2 is 50 and hence x_1 is the preferred action. However, the pessimist might assume that any finite chance of a zero pay-off is sufficient to deter him from that action – he takes certainties only and thus chooses x_2 despite its lower expected value. Such behaviour is often known as a max-min strategy since it effectively involves a comparison just of the minimum pay-offs to each action from which the maximum is selected. Conversely, we can look at the risk-lover's strategy from the same set of pay-offs but reverse the probabilities of y_1 and y_2, so that y_1 now occurs with a probability of 0.3 and the expected pay-off to x_1 is now only 30. For the risk-lover a finite chance of a high pay-off, however small that may be, can be an inducement to choose such a strategy.

Returning to our location choice example we might note here that there is considerable evidence from many areas of environmental and transport evaluation that individuals do apparently place quite high valuations on the existence of a choice option which they never use, simply because of the fear that it might not be there if they should need it. The car-owner who never uses the bus but locates near a bus route in case the car breaks down, the person who never visits an historic home or an area of scenic beauty but values their continued existence even to the extent of contributing voluntarily to their preservation are good examples of such behaviour. If these are widespread it does suggest that simple maximisation of an expected value will not suffice as an explanation of behaviour under uncertainty in a spatial situation where individuals may constantly hedge to avoid risk-bearing because the loss could be great even if its probability of occurring is very small.

The implications of this for the simple choice models of Chapter 3 are considerable. Our models of both transport and location choices were based on individuals being able to select unambiguously from a set of alternatives with known characteristics. All travel decisions are subject to major elements of risk, relative times of journeys by different modes are not known with accuracy, nor is the probability of obtaining a seat. It is true that for frequently made journeys such as commuting the traveller can construct a fairly accurate distribution of probable values for each such characteristic. However, it is not clear that simply replacing certain values by expected values is sufficient. For many workers it is not adequate to expect to arrive at work at 9 a.m. on average, since they might be required to be late on no more than 5 per cent or less of all mornings. Hence 9 a.m. must be at the ninety-fifth percentile of the distribution, meaning that the average arrival time must be much earlier. Thus it may well be the variance of a distribution rather than its mean or expected value which is a critical determinant of choice. However, such considerations will be much less important where there are no such constraints on arrival times and here expected values may be more relevant.

It would appear that there is no obvious *a priori* means of modifying choice models to allow for risks and uncertainties. The relevance of such considerations and the appropriate correction to use will vary from case to case. This remains an area where much work needs to be done and especially so for location choice. Here many characteristics will be subject to risk or uncertainty variations, particularly those relating to environmental features; and with no completely satisfactory way of dealing with such variations. What does seem likely, however, is that individuals will be motivated towards reducing such risks and uncertainties both in the interests of improving welfare and improving decision-making efficiency.

THEORIES OF SEARCH BEHAVIOUR

In any world of imperfect knowledge there will be uncertainty, but an economic agent can take actions to reduce uncertainty by identifying a quantifiable risk and to reduce risk by identifying less risky course of action. The implication is that the individual, before taking a decision, accumulates information to improve his decision-taking and learns from past experiences. However, acquiring knowledge is a costly operation, as anyone who has tried, for example, to learn fuller details of a local housing market would confirm. As each additional piece of information tends to add less and less to the individual's total knowledge such that it affects his decision, and hence his ultimate pay-off, less and less, there is obviously going to be a break-even point where the additional pay-off is just outweighed by the cost of search. What any person interested in a spatial market wishes to know is how much search will go on, when the optimal point of stopping the search occurs, and what is the loss of resources through search and wrong decisions in order that some evaluation of an improved information service can be undertaken.

We can only hope to sample a flavour of search theories here: much of the literature is of a very technical nature, which is to be expected for a decision-process which occurs through time, and indeed very little attention has yet been given to the problem of searching through both time and space. A great deal of the literature has been concerned with search in the labour market in an attempt to solve some of the questions about the nature and duration of unemployment and the relationship between this and the rate of change of wages. For our purposes and ease of exposition let us assume that we have a consumer planning a normal consumption activity, the general result can easily be extended to a travel or location problem or similar problems facing the producer.

In our analysis so far a consumer has always been faced with a known, predetermined price for a consumption good and based his level of consumption on this and his preference function. The simplest form of search model replaces the known price with a known distribution of prices from which the consumer can sample sequentially, the cost of each sample (the cost of search) being known and constant. In other words the consumer has sufficient information to know the distribution of prices charged, its mean, variance and so on, but he does not know what he would be charged at any particular shop. Assuming that there is a very large number of shops so that he cannot obtain complete information easily, the problem is to determine which shop to buy from. Since we need to assume for the moment that the search cost is a constant the sampling can be thought of as a series of telephone calls to each shop in turn. In this situation it can be shown that the optimal policy for the consumer is to determine a switchpoint or reservation price and reject all sample prices above this switchpoint, accepting any price which falls below it. This critical value is one which equates the marginal cost of a further search with its expected marginal return. Put more formally the problem is to determine an optimal stopping rule for a stochastic sequence of prices $X_1 \ldots \ldots X_n$ generated randomly and independently with a cumulative distribution function $F(X)$.

Let the price at the nth search be X_n, and the constant cost of each search be c, and let there be a sequence of prices $\bar{X}_n$ such that if $X_n \leq \bar{X}_n$ that price is accepted but if $X_n > \bar{X}_n$ it is rejected and the search continues. If the value of the search process under optimal conditions at the nth stage is given by V_n the acceptance of the nth offer leads to an expected gain, $G(X_n)$ of $E \operatorname{Max}[(X_n, X) - c]$. The consumer will stop searching if $V_n = G(X_n)$ and will clearly continue if $V_n = E(V_{n+1}) - c$ since the expected value of a further search is greater than that of the current stopping place by an amount at least equal to the additional cost of the extra search.

The distribution of $\bar{X}_n$ can be shown to satisfy,

$$c = \int_{\bar{X}_n}^{\infty} (X - \bar{X}_n) \, dF(X), \qquad (4.1)$$

which has certain interesting properties. If we assume an infinite search horizon then the switchpoint is constant. If the costs should change during the search process then the switchpoint will change, rising as costs rise and falling as costs fall, the optimal length of search thus shortening or lengthening accordingly.

These basic results can be modified to demonstrate the effects of more realistic assumptions, in particular we can discount future returns to allow for the loss of benefit from use of the purchase if a decision to buy is delayed to allow more search, we can place a finite horizon on the search, and we can relax the implicit assumption of risk neutrality to see what happens to the optimal policy when the nature of the distribution changes (i.e. search gets more risky). The final modifications will be critical for the spatial search case, an optimal policy when the distribution of prices is not known and when the cost of search is neither constant nor varying in a regular manner.

If we define a discounting factor $d = \dfrac{1}{1+r}$ where r is the appropriate rate of interest, this simply alters the expected gain to

$$G(X_n) = d[E(\operatorname{Max}(\bar{X}_n, X) - c)] \qquad (4.2)$$

and for the solution $\bar{X}_n$ will vary directly with the interest rate, the higher the interest rate the higher will be the switchpoint price and consequently the shorter the likely search. In the infinite time-horizon case the switchpoint was constant, but when we impose a finite time-horizon on the search process the reservation price does respond to the length of the search: in this case it will rise as the search proceeds, i.e. as we get nearer to the given horizon. This will be true because the expected value of each additional search will tend to fall as the number of possible remaining searches falls; and with constant search costs this will push up the optimal switchpoint price.

So far we have assumed that the consumer is indifferent (neutral) towards risk so that the decision to be made at each stage of the search involves the comparison of a certain return on the price available at that stage with an expected return from re-sampling – the optimal solution involving the·equation of these two. If, however, the consumer is averse to risk this will normally imply that he values the certain return more highly than an equivalent expected value. Consequently we can expect the switchpoint to be higher for a consumer who is more risk-averse and conversely one who enjoys the risks involved in the search has a reservation price accordingly lower.

The analysis has dealt with the comparative statics only to this stage. Now we must consider the effects of a dynamic change in the risks faced by the consumer. Firstly we need to define what is meant by risk or an increase in risk. Two alternative definitions have been proposed, each of which has rather different implications for the behaviour of the switchpoint (Rothschild and Stiglitz, 1970; Diamond and Stiglitz, 1974). Essentially increasing risk in a distribution relates to an increase in its variance since that is usually taken as a measure of the riskiness involved in sampling from a given distribution and obtaining a value within a particular range. When the variance is increased observations are, in effect, moved from the centre of the distribution to the tails, the mean remaining constant. However, we can distinguish between such a transformation of the distribution of prices as preserves the expected value of that distribution (a mean-preserving increase) and a transformation which preserves the expected *utility* derived from the distribution (mean-utility-preserving increase), whilst in each case increasing the proportion of observations in the tails of the price distribution. The importance of this distinction is that a risk-averter, in terms of utility, could prefer an increase in risk which preserves the expected value of the distribution since it increases the probability of finding a very low price and hence makes it more worth while for the consumer to wait for such a sample. As might be expected from this it is only for a mean-utility-preserving increase in risk that an unambiguous effect on the switchpoint can be identified; in our example it will fall for a risk-neutral consumer. For a mean-preserving increase the effect is ambiguous and the switchpoint could rise or fall depending on the nature of the new distribution of prices.

On the whole, therefore, defining riskiness in terms of the effect on expected utility gives us the likely result that in situations of higher risk the switchpoint will fall and hence the search is likely to be longer. This could, of course, be an important result when we consider the adjustment of individuals to changes in the spatial economy such as new transport systems changing the prices for a range of activities. The more frequently an activity is undertaken the less risky is the distribution and hence the shorter will be the adjustment sequence through search; for less frequent activities the adjustment sequence (in terms of the number of searches, not time) will be longer.

Now let us take the case of very infrequent activities, ones which have no known prior distribution. In such a situation the individual cannot determine immediately an optimum strategy based on an optimal reservation price – he has to gather information concerning the correct switchpoint from successive searches and adapt the search policy accordingly. In such a situation each successive sample from the distribution of prices not only leads to a decision whether to accept that offer but also to a decision whether to revise the distribution of prices. The usual approach to such a situation is in terms of Bayesian statistics where the consumer summarises what imperfect information he may have about a distribution in the form of a prior distribution, each additional piece of information is tested for consistency against this prior distribution and the parameters of the prior adjusted accordingly.

Unfortunately, in the case of unknown distributions it is not always possible to derive a switchpoint. If a prior distribution of prices is known, but only imperfectly, it is possible to derive optimal searches leading to the usual reservation-price property. If, however, nothing is known then it is possible to assume alternative prior distributions which give no such optimal switchpoint and accordingly no optimal strategy.

It is appropriate at this rather negative stage of development, where the introduction of complete uncertainty removes all order from the model, to cast one further doubt on the model. We can, it has been seen, develop consistent and powerful models of individual behaviour and choice under uncertainty but these have one important feature in common – the individual has a known and well-defined preference structure and utility function. It is quite conceivable that the individual does not know the nature of his utility function until he has sampled all the goods or all the characteristics which may enter into it. Some recent analysis has attempted to extend the idea of adaptive behaviour (which we shall consider in greater detail in Chapter 7) to the utility function itself, which is learned in a series of sub-optimising adaptations of behaviour (Cyert and De Groot, 1975). Fortunately, this is not destructive of the rest of decision theory but suggests that it may be possible to place it on a more rigorous foundation and explain many of the phenomena which behaviourist writers on markets have encountered.

It is relatively easy to move from a situation of constant search costs to incorporate cyclical effects into the model with the search cost inflating or deflating through time. However, the essence of search in a spatial environment is that the random sample of searches is itself randomly dispersed in space such that no regular pattern of search costs can be assumed. The individual's decision problem is, therefore, not just to choose an optimal stopping-point by deciding when the returns on a further search are just outweighed by its cost, but also to choose an optimal route to that point. If we assume that each sample point has a unique location in space then as well as the distribution of prices the individual faces a matrix of costs, C, each element of which, c_{ij}, represents the cost of moving from search point i to search point j, for example in terms of transport costs.

The seeking of optimal paths through networks is a well-established routine in both operations research and transport modelling (Haggett and Chorley, 1969) but such algorithms depend on either a constant, or at least a certain, outcome at each node of the network. Here we have only a random observation from a distribution of outcomes occurring at each destination or node of the network. The important question to be answered is the degree of interdependence between the distribution of outcomes and the optimal route strategy. In general it has been shown to be possible for the optimal route not to be changed by a mean-preserving spread of the distribution of outcomes, but not to demonstrate any stronger properties. A general solution involves complex programming techniques of either dynamic or recursive types, to which we shall return later in the book.

Given that there is no general solution to the choice of optimal route and optimal stopping-point problem it is not possible to formulate a policy in terms of a well-behaved reservation price or switchpoint as in the constant cost of search case. We find that the optimal order of search will differ according to the starting-point in that, for example, two identical people searching the same market and faced with the same known distribution of prices and the same costs of search between all pairs of points do not necessarily have the same optimal sequence of searching if they start from different initial positions. From any one geographical point they will not necessarily find it optimal to select the same subsequent sample point. An implication of this result is that it can be part of an optimal strategy to be observed moving apparently perversely – towards higher prices or lower pay-offs. Also the structure of the search costs will have an effect on the response of the switchpoint to changes in the degree of risk in the distribution but this may move either way and hence in a finite time-horizon the length of search may increase or decrease.

Optimal search theory in a spatial environment is thus an extremely complex problem – even those few tentative explorations of the problem which have been attempted involve techniques beyond the scope of this book. The conclusions from the theoretical simulations so far produced do have some important implications for spatial behaviour which need to be taken into account. The essence of search theories is that they decompose optimal behaviour patterns into a sequence of actions which add up to the best ultimate solution. It therefore emerges that when we observe individuals acting in space their immediate actions may appear irrational (non-optimal) when taken in isolation from the rest of the sequence. We shall have to exercise great care in defining the parameters of optimal behaviour in our final analysis and in specifying empirical models. The inclusion of non-constant search costs in spatial search accentuates this problem in that individuals may actually take decisions which are non-optimal as part of a long-run search problem as well as be observed in the process of short-run searching for optimal decisions. A particular case of this which has been the subject of some analysis is that of migration; the relocation of residence can be seen as part of a long-run job-search problem where people can be observed counter-migrating against a flow which would be implied by an examination of normal economic criteria such as relative wages.

MODELS OF SPATIAL CHOICE UNDER UNCERTAINTY

Despite the obvious importance of uncertainty in decision-making in a spatial environment this is an aspect of choice which has not received much attention from either transport or location modellers. We noted in Chapter 3 how the basic models of transport choice have concentrated on frequently-undertaken, familiar activities and that the transition to the less habitual activities of recreational travel would pose considerable problems. Even within the safer world of the work journey there appear to be problems, however. The literature on perception, particularly the perception of attributes of those choices not usually selected, suggests that there is not only uncertainty but considerable ignorance on the part of travellers. Not only are decision-makers not in full possession of all the facts relevant to the choice, so that their decision is subject to a degree of risk, but they often positively fail to obtain that information which could be obtained. Partly this is covered by our consideration of search theories, where it becomes clear that it is the perceived cost of acquiring extra information relative to the perception of potential loss from not having such information which is most relevant.

To some extent this has always been put down to either irrationality on the part of individuals or the sort of idiosyncrasy which lies at the base of the random utility model with its stochastic component in individuals' utility functions. The commonly taken view is that it does not matter if individuals are individually irrational in this sense so long as the stochastic element is truly random and assumed to be distributed with no pronounced bias such that collectively individuals are behaving as if rational.

Whilst little has yet been done to incorporate either uncertainty or search costs into the transport choice function, some interest has been shown in the related questions of mode captivity and habit. Many travellers are captive to a single mode of transport because of the simple unavailability of any alternative, but it has also been noted that individuals who have alternatives available which compare favourably, and even about which they have knowledge, still appear captive to one mode (Collings, 1974). This effect has not only been noted among individuals undertaking personal travel but also in the behaviour of freight shippers. To a large extent this factor may be accounted for by additional unmeasured attributes of the modes in question and it is to this end that additional work has been carried out on for example the definition of more precise measures of comfort and convenience (Hensher and McLeod, 1977).

Habit, however, might still play an important role in the determining of choice. The suggestion here is that it is inadequate to consider decision-makers as having smooth marginal response curves to stimuli as implied by the assumption of specific frequency distributions in most statistical analysis. In practice individuals only respond to substantial changes in relative characteristics in a manner better described by certain alternative statistical functions (Goodwin, 1977).

One further application of models involving some recognition of the problems of an uncertain world is in the area of spatial diffusion. The use of various randomising procedures such as the Monte Carlo process to simulate the spread of, for example, new techniques in agriculture was pioneered mainly by Hägerstrand (1967) and Wolpert (1965) and has become fairly widespread in geographical studies of the organisation of production. The main difficulty with these approaches is that they are based on purely random generations of events from certain known prior probabilities. Whilst they can simulate, often quite accurately, a spatial pattern of distribution of a particular phenomenon they lack the deterministic basis of our earlier models and are of limited use for either prediction or evaluation which have been seen so far as the primary goal of our spatial models of behaviour. Similarly the application of search models has thus far been restricted essentially to large-scale simulation exercises with aggregate data flows, but this latter technique does seem to offer on *a priori* grounds a better hope of coping with some of these important problems in a useful and practical way.

In this chapter we have attempted to consider how real-world phenomena such as uncertainty and ignorance can be incorporated into models of the decision process. In particular, it has been seen how much these are part of spatial economic decisions. However, it remains unclear just what the practical significance of these modifications is. On the one hand it seems unlikely that decision rules under uncertainty or for search can define fully optimising positions, at best they are likely to involve sub-optimising. On the other hand it is difficult to see how search models, for example, can be used to predict precise actions since they depend essentially on randomised simulations. We are therefore in neither a Löschian world of spatial optima nor the more pragmatic world of the simple transport or location modeller. It would appear that the models discussed in this chapter have rather more limited scope than this but are none the less of considerable importance since they offer an attempt to *understand* rather than *explain* observed behaviour. They enable us to understand why the apparently rather contradictory behaviour frequently observed in spatial economics is not necessarily irrational and suggest the . importance of considering imperfect adjustments to changing situations, to which we shall return in Chapter 7.

GUIDE TO FURTHER READING

The basic analysis of choices involving risk can be found in von Neumann and Morgenstern (1944), Friedman and Savage (1948), Alchian (1953) and Arrow (1970). There are useful reviews in Baumol (1977), Bacharach (1976) and Green (1976). Useful introductions to theories of search and behaviour under changing conditions are Rothschild and Stiglitz (1970), Diamond and Stiglitz (1974), Rothschild (1973), Kohn and Shavell (1974) and Lippman and McCall (1976), and an extension to consider spatial aspects in Treble (1976).

REFERENCES

Alchian, A. A. (1953), 'The meaning of utility measurement', *American Economic Review*, 43, 26–50.
Arrow, K. J. (1970), *Essays in the Theory of Risk Bearing* (Chicago: Markham).
Bacharach, M. (1976), *Economics and the Theory of Games* (London: Macmillan).
Baumol, W. J. (1977), *Economic Theory and Operations Analysis*, 4th ed. (Englewood Cliffs, N. J.: Prentice-Hall).
Collings, J. J. (1974), 'The application of behavioural mode-choice models to leisure travel', *Environment and Planning A*, 6, 169–83.
Cyert, R. M., and De Groot, M. H. (1975), 'Adaptive utility', in R. H. Day and T. Groves (eds.), *Adaptive Economic Models* (New York: Academic Press).
Diamond, P. A., and Stiglitz, J. E. (1974), 'Increases in risk and risk aversion', *Journal of Economic Theory*, 8, 337–60.
Friedman, M., and Savage, L. J. (1948), 'The utility analysis of choices involving risk', *Journal of Political Economy*, 56, 279–304.
Goodwin, P. B. (1977), 'Habit and hysteresis in mode choice', *Urban Studies*, 14, 95–8.
Green, H. A. J. (1976), *Consumer Theory*, rev. ed. (London: Macmillan).
Hägerstrand, T. (1967), *Innovation Diffusion as a Spatial Process*, tr. A. R. Pred (Chicago: Chicago U.P.).
Haggett, P., and Chorley, R. J. (1969), *Network Analysis in Geography* (London: Arnold).
Hensher, D. A., and McLeod, P. B. (1977), 'Towards an integrated

approach to the identification and evaluation of the transport determinants of travel choices', *Transportation Research*, 11, 77–93.

Kohn, M. G., and Shavell, S. (1974), 'The theory of search', *Journal of Economic Theory*, 9, 93–123.

Lippman, S., and McCall, J. J. (1976), 'The economics of job search: a survey', *Economic Inquiry*, 14, 155–89, 347–68.

Rothschild, M. (1973), 'Models of market organisation with imperfect information: a survey', *Journal of Political Economy*, 81, 1283–308.

Rothschild, M., and Stiglitz, J. E. (1970), 'Increasing risk: I. A definition', *Journal of Economic Theory*, 2, 225–43.

Treble, J. G. (1976), 'A spatial search theory of migration', *Hull Economic Research Papers*, 13.

von Neumann, J., and Morgenstern, O. (1944), *The Theory of Games and Economic Behaviour* (Princeton, N.J.: Princeton U.P.).

Wolpert, J. (1965), 'Behavioural aspects of the decision to migrate', *Papers and Proceedings of the Regional Science Association*, 15, 159–72.

5 Conflicts in Spatial Behaviour

The models of spatial behaviour developed so far have assumed that we can examine the behaviour of individual travellers, households or firms as if they were totally independent of all other decision-makers in the economy. Each individual decision-maker faces a set of influencing variables, the values of which are determined as states of the world, which he cannot alter. In the first instance he was assumed to have perfect knowledge of all these values and to take his decisions accordingly, but even when we introduced elements of uncertainty these were seen simply as a lack of the necessary knowledge of the true state of the world. The individual could gain by playing appropriate strategies but could not affect the actual outcome in terms of changing the final state of the world.

Now we must drop this assumption and consider what happens when individuals come into conflict with other individuals, when by their actions and the strategy played they can actually affect the outcome, and hence when they become themselves active determinants of the values taken by determining variables of behaviour. In this chapter we first of all consider in theoretical terms how we can introduce such factors and then turn to analyse some of the more important conflicts which arise in the various dimensions of spatial behaviour with which we are concerned. In the final part of this chapter we consider some of the responses to conflict which emerge and the role of coalitions and collusion in the spatial economy.

THE ANALYSIS OF ECONOMIC CONFLICT

In many ways the whole rationale of economic analysis is one of conflict. The allocation of resources between competing and conflicting uses is achieved by the determination of a market clearing price. Our interest here will centre on those conflicts which are not resolved by the workings of a perfect market, those conflicts which cause the achieved outcome or pay-offs of particular economic actions to differ from the expected.

We have already approached the problem of conflict and one of the tools for its analysis in our discussion of uncertainty. There uncertainty of an outcome was associated with variations in pay-offs due to variations in natural or uncontrollable phenomena. Variations in the weather may affect the benefits to be derived from a day out in the country, variations in the level of stocking by different stores could lead to uncertainty in the consumer being able to buy a particular commodity. The type of conflict which we shall introduce here is a more objective conflict of interests between economic agents such that there is a conscious trade-off between each one's actions and the pay-offs derived by each of the others. Decision-making in such a situation is not just a question of maximising a known objective function subject to known constraints but is a game of strategy.

In the analysis of uncertainty we saw how the pay-off from a particular action can be expressed as a vector of pay-offs according to the probabilities of each of a range of possible outcomes. Earlier, in Chapter 2, we showed how an individual relating any single decision to all other decisions he has to take could form a decision matrix of pay-offs to form an optimal sequence of strategies. Hence we can easily make the transition to a game situation between two or more economic agents, each of whom perceives a vector of pay-offs associated with any specific choice, each element of which depends on the corresponding decision of the other agent(s). Of course, since the decision-maker does not know the action of his rival(s) he can only operate on the basis of probabilities – attempts to read the mind of the opponent.

Assume that an individual has a choice between two alternatives, O_1 and O_2. The reaction of another individual to the choice that he makes can also be one of two actions, E_1 and E_2, and whichever combination of action and reaction occurs will affect the pay-off. Hence the decision matrix can be written as below with appropriate pay-offs, x_{ij},

$$
\begin{array}{ccc}
 & E_1 & E_2 \\
O_1 & x_{11} & x_{12} \\
O_2 & x_{21} & x_{22}
\end{array}
$$

There will be various classes of outcome to this problem. An unambiguous choice of O_1 would occur if, for example, $x_{11} > x_{21}$, $x_{12} > x_{22}$, since regardless of the reaction, E_1 or E_2, strategy O_1 always gives the greatest pay-off and can be said to be dominant. If one strategy does not dominate in this way, say $x_{11} > x_{21}$ and $x_{11} > x_{12}$ but

$x_{22} > x_{12}$ and $x_{22} > x_{21}$, then clearly the likely reaction, E_1 or E_2, will determine the correct strategy; if E_1 occurs then O_1 is correct, if E_2 occurs then O_2 is correct.

Now it is fairly easy to deal with all the possible combinations of values in a two-by-two matrix to determine the appropriate strategies on the basis of the likely state of events. What we require before being able to tackle more realistic problems is a general principle to deal with situations involving many alternative strategies and many alternative reactions.

Let us first of all consider two extreme strategies, those of extreme optimism and extreme pessimism. An optimist is a decision-maker who looks simply for the best outcome from any series of situations in the belief that the final outcome will always favour him. He simply looks for the maximum pay-off and decides accordingly. If the ranking of pay-offs in our example were $x_{11} > x_{22} > x_{21} > x_{12}$, the optimist unambiguously selects option O_1 since it would yield the maximum pay-off, x_{11}, even though further examination shows that it could also yield the minimum pay-off, x_{12}, if E_2 were to occur. Treating the strategy probabilistically the optimist examines each alternative choice (row of the matrix) in turn, identifies the maximum pay-off and assigns a value of unity to it. This therefore becomes the expected value of that choice and he simply chooses between alternatives on the basis of the maximum expected pay-off.

The pessimist, on the other hand, is always on the lookout for failure rather than success and assigns the highest probability to the lowest pay-off for each strategy. The expected value is therefore given by the lowest pay-off for each choice and the alternatives will be compared on this basis, the choice being with the highest of these minimum values; and hence this pessimistic strategy has become known as the max-min. Since the minimum pay-off from O_2 is x_{21} and from O_1 is x_{12} and $x_{21} > x_{12}$ the pessimist chooses O_2.

Such a bald strategy may not appear a likely one in most situations. The crude assigning of probabilities of one or zero according to the individual's optimism or lack of it, even in a state of complete uncertainty, seems somewhat far-fetched. Suppose, for example, the values of the pay-offs in our example were:

Case 1	E_1	E_2
O_1	1000	150
O_2	175	200

This satisfies our assumed ordering of pay-offs but whilst our max-max strategy optimist is on the right track the max-min pessimist is making a great mistake unless the probability of E_1 occurring is very low.

Case 2 on the other hand is one which does not favour the optimist.

Case 2	E_1	E_2
O_1	200	10
O_2	175	190

Here the probability of E_1 occurring must be quite high before the expected value of the pay-off from O_1 is high enough to be larger than that from O_2.

Even in a world of uncertainty the majority of decision-makers are unlikely to be such extremists, especially if aware of the full significance of the pay-off matrix as in our two cases above. Most individuals have some prior expectation of probabilities for most decisions they take. A simple assumption in absence of any knowledge is to assign equal probabilities to all possible outcomes. In our two cases we would assign probabilities of 0.5 to E_1 and E_2 in each case, leading to the following expected values of pay-off:

	Case 1	*Case 2*
O_1	575	105
O_2	187.5	182.5

Hence we would choose O_1 in Case 1 and O_2 in Case 2.

Obviously we can also determine the probabilities which would need to be assigned to the two outcomes in each case, which would just cause us to alter the final choice, that value which would render the pay-offs equal and hence lead to a switch of strategy. In Case 1 the probability of E_1 could fall to less than 0.06 before O_2 is as good as O_1, but in Case 2 the switchpoint would come with the probability of E_1 at about 0.88, that is when the probability of E_2 falls to about 0.12. This switchpoint approach enables us to consider the sensitivity of the strategy to uncertainties in the outcome: as long as some confidence interval can be placed about the probabilities used potential changes in the optimal strategy can be assessed.

An alternative way of combining the outcomes without the need to assign probabilities is in terms of a regret matrix. In this we look at the likely loss from being wrong. For example in Case 1 the individual chooses O_1 in the belief that E_1 will prevail, but if it does not and E_2 holds he sees that he could have done better by choosing O_2 and his loss or regret is $x_{22} - x_{12} = 50$. Similarly the pessimist who chose O_2 in the belief that E_2 would arise has a regret of 825 if E_1 comes about. For our two cases we can write regret matrices as follows:

	Case 1			*Case 2*	
	E_1	E_2		E_1	E_2
O_1	0	50	O_1	0	180
O_2	825	0	O_2	25	0

Like the max-min pessimist the pessimistic regretter will look for the worst outcome, here represented by the maximum regret from any strategy. He then sets about identifying the strategy which minimises this maximum possible loss – a min-max strategy – and chooses O_1 in Case 1 and O_2 in Case 2, much closer to the probability-based expected value outcome. If probabilities are available the regret matrix can be refined further to give expected values of regret.

So far our examples assume that the decision-maker is playing against an unknown but static environment but now we must look a little more deeply into the problem. Let us recall the nature of the decisions which interest us. The pay-off from a travel decision may depend on decisions taken by other road or public transport users – the greater the pay-off to one decision-maker the less the pay-off may be to another. Similarly for a location decision we must take into account the effects on, and the reactions of, rival users of that location. In other words the normal situation is not one of fighting a constant reaction but rather fighting a variable reaction, one which is governed by that decision-maker's own pay-offs.

In this situation our individual knows that if in Case 1 he chooses strategy O_1, his rival will choose E_2, in which case the first individual's optimum choice is O_2. However a choice of O_2 would lead to an optimum choice of E_1 by the rival. We assume throughout this example that there is a constant total pay-off such that a high value to person 1 means a low value to person 2. Such a situation can be characterised as a game, various classes of which can be noted.

The first characteristic of a game is the number of players: the critical distinction is between two-person games, where there is a direct conflict between the parties, and games with more than two players, in which although conflict may clearly exist it is also possible, and often optimal, for groups of two or more players to collude and secure a common advantage against other players. Secondly, there is a difference between games with a constant sum, of which one of the commonest forms is the zero-sum game, and those where the total pay-off to all players is variable according to their actions. The key feature of a non-constant sum game is that all the players may collude to gain an advantage. Thirdly, it is important to distinguish between games which have an equilibrium solution and those which do not. Those with an equilibrium or saddle point mean that a stable set of decisions can be taken by the various parties to the game. If such a solution cannot be found, such a satisfactory set of decisions cannot be taken and there will always be an incentive for players to change the decision subsequently.

These alternatives and the path to an equilibrium solution are best illustrated by an example. We start with a simple two-person zero-sum game situation as illustrated in Table 5.1. Here the two players A and B each have three possible choices labelled A(1), A(2) etc. leading to a pay-off matrix for A as shown in the table. Since the game is assumed to be zero-sum the pay-off to B is minus the pay-off to A and hence Table 5.1 can also be interpreted as a regret matrix for B.

TABLE 5.1

	B(1)	B(2)	B(3)	Min
A(1)	7	3	4	3
A(2)	4	−5	3	−5
A(3)	−4	0	1	−4
Max	7	3	4	

The appropriate minimum and maximum values for each row and column are shown in the table and hence we can apply the pessimistic view to both A's and B's decisions by use of max-min and min-max regret strategies respectively. From this it is easy to see that A will choose A(1) to maximise the minimum possible pay-off and B will choose B(2) to minimise his maximum regret value. Since these two coincide with the value 3, the game has a stable equilibrium solution of A(1), B(2), each player's choice is vindicated and he has no desire to change his selection.

A very small modification to this structure can destabilise this game, however, as illustrated in Table 5.2. Here A will still choose A(1) on the max-min rule but B is now undecided between B(2) and B(3). Whichever choice B makes will not lead to a solution since the min-max regret value is not equal to the max-min value for A. If A were to choose A(1) then B will want to choose B(3), but if he did A would be better off by choosing A(2), in which case B would prefer B(2) and hence A is back to choosing A(1). Since both are expected to reason in this way neither can choose rationally and whichever choice is made is immediately seen to be wrong.

TABLE 5.2

	B(1)	B(2)	B(3)	Min
A(1)	7	3	1	1
A(2)	4	−5	3	−5
A(3)	−4	0	1	−4
Max	7	3	3	

It is always possible to generate a solution to such a zero-sum game which is not strictly determined by allowing the players to mix strategies. If A is able to play some combination of A(1), A(2) and A(3) with probabilities p_1, p_2, p_3 ($p_1 + p_2 + p_3 = 1$) respectively and B can play a mixture of his strategies with probabilities q_1, q_2, q_3 ($q_1 + q_2 + q_3 = 1$) it is always possible to find values of p_i and q_i ($i = 1, 2, 3$) which transform the pay-offs of Table 5.2 to a matrix which is strictly determined (i.e. has a stable solution). Mixed strategies may often be difficult to interpret where some alternatives are mutually exclusive. It is possible for a firm choosing optimal locations for distributions centres to opt for two smaller depots in different locations, for example, but not usually for a household to have two residences or a person to travel simultaneously by two modes of transport. However, treated sequentially people do change strategies. Presumably one reason for multiple home-ownership is that no single location is ideal for the desired range of activities. People alternate between modes of transport and frequently mix modes on single journeys. This could therefore explain the otherwise difficult observation that individuals make a different choice from the same set on different occasions even when no other factors change.

The zero-sum game discussed above is only a special case of the constant-sum game and the same principles apply to the finding of stable solutions to such games since the players have only a given sum to divide between them as a pay-off; all such games can therefore be transformed into a zero-sum game. If we allow the sum to vary, however, then, even with two players, the situation changes. Table 5.3 illustrates a non-constant-sum game in which the pay-offs, written here as regret values, are expressed in pairs for each pair of strategy. The first value is the regret value to A, the second is that to B.

TABLE 5.3

	B(1)	B(2)
A(1)	−10, −10	−20, −2
A(2)	−2, −20	−20, −20

This game is derived from the well-known Prisoners' Dilemma where the regret values are lengths of sentences dependent on confess or non-confess strategies corresponding to (2) and (1) respectively in Table 5.3. Here we see that each player sees his own best course of action as strategy (2) as long as his opponent can be guaranteed to take strategy (1). But of course this cannot be guaranteed, they both choose (2) and maximise not only their own losses but also the total loss. If, however, the players could collude, with full knowledge of the pay-offs, they would see that A(1), B(1) is a better position, not only than A(2), B(2) but also than either of the other two positions, since the total regret is least. There is no way that they would agree to say A(2), B(1) because even if A paid B compensation he cannot compensate him to a position B would prefer to A(1), B(1) without making himself worse off than at A(1), B(1).

In a two-person variable-sum game collusion between players can leave both better off, in a three-or-more-person game all the players are not necessarily better off as a result of collusion since this can take place to their mutual advantage between sub-groups of players with a view to gaining at the expense of other players or groups. Here interest centres on the optimal coalition structure which will emerge. The set of such solutions is known as the core of the game. Since the economy as a whole can be viewed as a trading game this device of coalitions and the concept of the core is of considerable use in examining whether a particular set of circumstances can lead to a stable equilibrium for the economy as a whole. This is beyond the scope of this book but its value is such as to make it well worth introducing to our consideration of the structure of local economies.

We now have a basic tool-kit to consider questions of conflict and their resolution either through the establishing of an equilibrium situation or by collusion and the formation of coalitions. The importance of the game theoretic approach is once again not one of providing neat, deterministic solutions to decisions or behaviour but in understanding why many observed actions may in fact have been made. Once we move away from the independent, atomistic decision-maker we need to recognise the importance of strategy in decision-making. There is no reason why the observed behaviour of the decision-maker should always conform to a predetermined optimal pattern – the great advantage of the game theory framework is that it enables us to focus on these more realistic factors in decision-making.

CONFLICTS IN SPATIAL CHOICE – EQUILIBRIUM

It is apparent from the abstract discussion of the preceding section that we need to consider conflict under several headings according to the type of game situation implicit. The main features of interest to us are, however, whether the game is a simple constant-sum game with an equilibrium solution which we shall consider in this section, or whether it is a non-constant-sum situation which will lead to forms of collusion which we consider in the next section of this chapter.

Conflicts in economics are essentially conflicts over the use of resources, either in terms of the ownership of property rights, and hence the rights to determine questions of use, or in terms of conflicts arising during consumption. Information is typically conveyed by means of prices which reflect scarcity values and thus enable the various potentially conflicting parties to reach stable equilibrium decisions. So far we are only equipped to talk about conflicts within a single sector such as travel decisions, that is about what is usually described as the achievement of partial equilibrium. Conflicts which cross sectoral boundaries we shall have to defer until we have discussed the general equilibrium of the economy.

A number of separate games will be apparent within each sector. The basic game is that between producers and consumers. We are interested essentially in whether the market will clear in the sense that the amount supplied will exactly equal the amount demanded at the ruling price. Secondly, there will be a secondary game played between producers over the market share each achieves. In a world of perfect competition this is a trivial game since no producer has any worthwhile strategy other than to produce at optimal levels of output or not at all. Thirdly, there may be a game situation between consumers in which they attempt to secure an advantage over rival consumers for a given supply, again a situation which will not prevail under perfect competition.

To discuss conflicts between producers and consumers and the possibility of achieving sectoral equilibrium requires us first to have some knowledge of production or cost functions for the various sectors. We do not have the space here to enter into a detailed discussion of this question for all our various concerns but a fairly brief consideration can yield a number of worthwhile insights which will be helpful.

Transport

The study of transport costs reveals a number of clear factors. First of all the production of transport services requires typically a very large capital outlay in infrastructure. This infrastructure is subject to fairly dramatic economies of scale such that larger transport corridors cost less per track-kilometre or per lane-kilometre to build. Thomson (1974) has quoted figures relating to 1967–68 of £49,000 per track-kilometre for a four-track railway compared with £75,000 per track-kilometre for two tracks, a saving of over one third. For motorways the saving is a little less in proportion, at £105,000 per lane-kilometre for a twin four-lane road against £147,000 for a twin two-lane road. Hence any transport authority, public or private, has a cost incentive to focus traffic on to as few large links of a network as possible from the point of view of fixed costs. This comparison is emphasised if maintenance costs are included.

The second element of costs is that of terminal costs – the cost of providing access for travellers or shippers to and from the transport network and connections between links of the same network or between different networks. Here there is greater variety between transport modes: terminal costs for aircraft or railways tend to be a rather higher proportion of total costs than for other modes. However, as with infrastructure costs there are substantial economies of scale to be derived, whether we are referring to airports, railway marshalling yards, highway interchanges or car parks.

The third element of transport costs is of haulage costs, the cost of actually moving people or goods along a network. This also consists of two basic elements, the capital costs of vehicles ranging from aircraft to railway locomotives to trucks to cars to bicycles, and the traction costs, the cost of actually propelling the vehicle along the network. Here again there are economies of scale expressed in relation to some standardised measure of capacity such as seat-kilometres or tonne-kilometres available per unit of input. This is often most telling when comparisons are made across modes of transport with reference to the now critical energy input, where Pryke and Dodgson (1975) have reported figures for estimated seat-miles per gallon (s.m.p.g.). Private cars are the least efficient at 80–160 s.m.p.g., long-distance trains intermediate at about 350 s.m.p.g., and urban buses (525) and underground trains (630) the most efficient. For freight the differences are less pronounced with larger lorries achieving 120–150 ton-m.p.g. and rail 120–175 ton-m.p.g. All of these comparisons are based on available capacities and differences might be more pronounced if actual work done was compared, allowing for capacity utilisation and occupancy rates.

Thus we have a picture of basically downward-sloping cost curves over a considerable range of output for the provision of most transport services. The optimum choice of mode for particular traffic will usually depend on the extent to which the various economies in infrastructure or vehicle size can be brought into play, since there is one important element in the costs of most public transport operators which we have not referred to, that of labour costs. Because of the considerable scale economies which can be reaped from other inputs the labour input is a very significant component of average costs and whilst considerable productivity advances have been made both in terms of reducing the number of staff per vehicle and eliminating skill requirements by automatic control of many functions there is a limit to this process.

But what of the organisation of transport provision? What role does that play in the relevant supply equation? The critical distinction is between those modes which control both infrastructure and haulage, such as rail, and those which only provide haulage on a public infrastructure. The dominance of infrastructure in the scale economies means that large firms are bound to emerge in the provision of rail transport services, but where an operator does not provide infrastructure there is little evidence of large economies of scale in the size of fleet operated beyond quite modest levels of five to ten vehicles. This finding is evidenced by data for both bus and truck operators. The provision of road infrastructure, particularly in urban areas, has been almost exclusively the preserve of public authorities although this is more likely to be for social than simple economic reasons, as we shall see presently. In the sphere of inter-urban roads privately operated toll roads are in widespread use in many countries, such as the United States, Italy, France and Spain, although these are usually only operated on the basis of publicly-controlled concessions.

A further important feature is the widespread use of owner-operated private vehicles in both passenger transport, with the private car, and freight transport, with the own-account haulage operator. The reasons for choice of such a mode for a particular journey have already been discussed in Chapter 3 but there is the further question of vehicle ownership, the reasons which persuade a particular decision-maker to include this option amongst his choices. The explanation and forecasting of vehicle ownership is a complex and often hazardous procedure as evidenced by the frequent lack of success in many such exercises. Our concern here is more with the consequences of that decision, since there is no doubt that once given a capital stake in the vehicle this changes substantially the relative costs of various modes for individual journeys. Individuals are frequently comparing costs in which the recovery of sunk capital is assessed on a totally different basis: the procedure used by the average motorist is very different from that of a public transport operator, road or rail, publicly or privately owned. Such distortions have implications not only for choice of mode of transport but also for equilibrium in transport markets.

We have covered in this brief review the main determinants of transport costs but we have not made it clear what the relevant unit of output is in order that the possibility of equilibrium can be assessed. Individuals demand transport fairly clearly in terms of complete journeys, travel from A to B or the consignment of a given load from A to B. Transport suppliers, except for those who provide their own haulage, do not supply transport on such terms except under special arrangements such as contracted hire of vehicles. Public transport agencies normally offer a given capacity of seats or tonnage over a fixed route which only incidentally coincides with the journey demanded. Typically their output is measured as vehicle-kilometres operated multiplied by vehicle capacity, during a given period. In such circumstances it is difficult to consider equilibrium of demand and supply in the usual way: suppliers provide a network of services which approximates to the desired travel patterns of individuals, subject to the constraints of the production and cost relationships. Similarly, as we have already discussed, individual journey-patterns will be altered in terms of destinations, frequency and timing by the characteristics of available transport modes.

The net result of this evidence is to suggest that such equilibrium of demand and supply which does emerge in the transport sector is a somewhat artificial one. There will be an important tendency towards concentration to reap the available economies of scale, giving strong impetus to clustering of origins and destinations to avoid excessive transport costs. The effects which changing transport technologies have had on the development of city structure has been graphically portrayed by Schaeffer and Sclar (1975), and not least the problems which this influence has brought in its wake.

Land and Property

Turning now to the market in land and property a number of striking similarities can be observed with the transport situation. As with transport, fixed costs are dominant, possibly to an even greater extent. We also have considerable problems in defining the correct units of supply and demand, and major difficulties with different patterns of tenure and ownership. A very high proportion of the cost of housing is

absorbed by the capital costs of its initial building: subsequent maintenance and other current costs are small in comparison with the recurrent
costs of debt servicing implied by the initial cost. Similar considerations
also apply to building for commercial use. Most building is financed by
loan capital, although it is interesting to note that a large proportion of
new building is speculative in the sense that it is undertaken by a
developer without a specific purchaser in view, the majority of buyers
purchasing a finished item and not bearing production risks themselves,
in the same way as with most goods. The main question of relevance is
whether the final users of buildings take over these risks by outright
purchase of the building or simply rent use of the building without any
ownership rights (although of course many now have considerable rights
as tenants).

One of the major difficulties is the ideal unit of measurement. Clearly
there is no such thing as a standard housing unit or standard office unit.
To some extent a similar situation to that faced in transport exists in that
individuals tend to demand complete units, a house, a factory, etc.,
whereas developers produce a rather more abstract item in the form of
floor space. However, at least the finished product is clearly identifiable
in the case of buildings, and whilst a given capital investment in transport
may have a very wide variety of uses this is less so in the short term with
buildings.

Turning to the final structure of costs we are particularly interested in
the existence of scale economies. Technical economies do obviously
exist in building such that average costs per unit of space fall over quite a
large range. Hence developments involving high densities are usually
cheaper per unit than those offering low densities. This is partly due to
the effect of land costs but since these typically account for only a very
small proportion, around 5 per cent, of total costs there must also be
significant economies in the direct building costs. These also apply
whether high-rise or high-density low-rise style building is used. There is
a fairly pronounced limit to these economies, which are essentially ones
relating to the fixed costs of service provision, and consequently there
may be critical thresholds of size producing a rather irregular pattern of
scale economies. This situation means that it is quite possible for there to
be several feasible equilibrium sizes of development.

The critical feature of the supply of buildings for the achievement of
equilibrium is the length of time taken from the decision to supply to the
building being ready for occupation: this means that any market will be
very slow to adjust and accordingly very difficult to observe at a given
point of time. There are various other reasons to do with planning and

building controls which may also be of relevance here, but these can be more properly discussed after we have introduced externality problems.

Spatial Competition

We have spent some time discussing the producer–consumer relationships of normal market action in considerable detail since the question of market equilibrium is a critical one. We can now consider producer–producer and consumer–consumer conflicts in rather less detail.

Producer–producer conflicts are essentially about the achieving of an optimal level of production without a single producer or group of producers achieving an excess of economic power, in effect the level of competition within the markets. Whilst we shall not discuss this in great detail, only needing for our purposes to draw out some of the more relevant conclusions, this particular issue is one of rather greater importance than this treatment might imply. Fortunately substantial treatments of the problem, notably by Greenhut (1970), do exist; possibly rather more on this aspect of spatial economics has been written than on most others.

The problem essentially derives out of the old issue of market areas and the extent to which in a spatial economy the natural tendency would be towards one of monopolistic influence. The classic treatment of this question is in Hotelling's now famous example of the beach ice-cream salesmen (1929). An optimal distribution of two ice-cream salesmen on a linear beach with uniformly distributed customers is for each to be at a distance one quarter of the total length of the beach from each end. This location minimises total travelling costs for the public and is therefore Pareto-optimal. The ice-cream salesmen are, however, motivated by the desire to increase their market shares, each induced to move towards the centre in order to capture some of the other's market. This process of trying to capture a larger share of the total can only reach an equilibrium distribution when each is at the centre of the beach. From this result we can deduce that equilibrium locations are inclined to be Pareto-inefficient. When the number of salesmen is increased the problem changes and it is interesting to note that, firstly, spatial equilibrium is less likely to be achieved in a linear market since there is usually an incentive to 'leapfrog' over one's competitors; but, secondly, that the resultant distribution more nearly approximates to the optimal.

Whilst the existence of space in markets does tend to produce local monopolies, in that a firm in a particular location is protected from the competition of his next nearest neighbours by the transport costs necessary to compete, a further question is whether that monopoly power can be eroded. The traditional view has tended to be that with free entry the monopoly power of firms is limited: by locating on the market area boundary of two existing firms a new entrant captures part of each market and reduces the existing firms' profits. Logically new entry could continue until all profits above normal were eliminated. The fact that this does not happen can be ascribed to imperfections in the market mechanism – the monopoly power exercised by firms in a spatial economy is seen as largely due to imperfect information.

This view has only been seriously challenged recently in a series of important papers by Eaton and Lipsey (1977, 1978), who have attempted to rework most of the standard neoclassical theory of the firm with the addition of space. The critical point in their analysis is the explicit recognition that any spatial concentration of production, whatever the spatial distribution of demand, depends on the existence of increasing returns to scale over the relevant range of output. If increasing returns to scale exist then there must be a critical minimum size of plant which a new entrant must be able to attain before entry can hope to be profitable. The extent to which the new entrant can undercut his rivals even when he has a spatial (locational) advantage is thus limited. Most important, however, is the limit to new entry. In the traditional model this is logically, but unrealistically, when there is an infinite number of infinitely small producers evenly distributed spatially. In the revised model the minimum size condition ensures the existence of spatial monopoly power and at a level of profits above normal, not because of imperfect information in the spatial economy but because of the nature of the production function itself.

One further point emerging from this view of the spatial organisation of markets is that it also suggests that the relevant responses are not smooth and continuous. Because of the minimum constraints on new entrants existing firms may have considerable freedom over pricing and output decisions, and hence a wide range of potential profit levels, without invoking retaliatory action from new entrants. Their strategy may thus be more concerned with preserving market areas *vis-à-vis* existing firms. Since existing firms have power relative to potential entrants much will depend on the number of firms in the industry. In practice a wide range of solutions may be possible, each of which is stable, the production conditions only determining the minimum size for profitable operation. It is in this indeterminate world that we can see the need for a game theory approach but also the difficulty in predicting both what will occur and what should occur in an optimal situation.

Consumer–consumer conflicts are, if one believes in consumer sovereignty, the nub of the market allocational system since it is consumers' conflicts over demands for goods that determine the allocation both of those goods and of resources to produce them. Consumers' conflicts are based on the assumption of two characteristics, firstly their command over resources with which goods can be exchanged, primarily money but also time, and secondly, the notion that in consuming a particular unit of a commodity any one individual can prevent all others from its consumption. These assumptions define the private good and are usually referred to as the properties of exclusion and rivalness respectively. In equilibrium we know from conventional economic theory that prices must adjust such that there is no frustrated demand: consumers who have both a willingness to buy a particular commodity and the relevant resources with which to do so can neither be excluded from the market nor lose their prospective purchase to others.

If this situation does not obtain then there remains a latent conflict within the market. If some consumers are not excluded by price but cannot purchase there is implicitly a rivalry between consumers if any other form of allocation by rationing or queueing takes place. The problem of matching spatial supply with spatial demands is an obvious source of this type of conflict. If we just consider the two sectors which we dealt with in greater detail earlier in this section we can see clearly how it will be very difficult to effect allocation without violation of the exclusion or rivalness principles. Transport involves consumption simultaneously with production and it is therefore extremely difficult to fix a market clearing price in advance of actual production, leading to the possibility of queueing and congestion. Similarly the fixity of land makes it exceedingly difficult to avoid rivalry between potential users over specific sites since production of that site cannot be increased to cater for any excess of demand.

Our general conclusion from these various considerations of the structure of spatial markets, both markets for normal goods and services in a spatial economy and those for specifically spatial activities such as land use and transport, is that equilibrium is relatively unlikely to be achieved and that some latent conflicts will exist within the economy. Our next task is, therefore, to consider these conflicts which are not resolved by the market, their effects on the structure of the economy and how they can be resolved in the interests of removing any implicit losses of welfare.

CONFLICTS IN SPATIAL CHOICE – EXTERNALITIES AND DISEQUILIBRIUM

Reference back to our abstract model of conflict and equilibrium tells us that there are two basic reasons for the non-achievement of a stable solution value, a conflict in optimal strategies in a fairly simple constant-sum game or the existence of a non-constant sum to the game.

The former is more easily dealt with since it only implies that the pay-off matrix as currently constructed for the pure strategies given has no solution. This is the situation which would exist if there were, for example, excess demand for a particular item and hence a reconsideration of the various strategies in the game is necessary. If a game such as that in Table 5.2 (p. 90 above) involves exactly three available strategies to each party and no others, then the solution cannot be found in inventing another strategy. In these circumstances the solution can be found by mixing strategies as discussed earlier. The key factor is the time taken to search for the optimal mix of strategies which determines the game. Conflicts are thus a short-term phenomenon which will be eliminated when an appropriate period for identifying the correct mix of strategies has elapsed.

Non-constant-sum games are a rather different proposition since these cannot usually be solved by a simple search for appropriate strategies and may instead settle at an apparent equilibrium which is not, however, optimal. Optimality in this case involves us looking not just at the individual behaviour and pay-offs of each participant in the game in question but at the total pay-offs to all participants, which we may term the social pay-off. Individual economic agents can in isolation only take decisions with reference to the private pay-off, since this is all that is perceived in the absence of the extra information which would come either from collusion with other interested parties or from additional information provided by a 'social' organisation such as a government. This extra information, which may often take the form of penalties such as a tax, causes the individual to perceive the full social pay-off as if it were a private decision and thus take decisions which are both individually and socially optimal.

There are two basic cases of divergence of social from private pay-offs which are relevant, those of externalities and public goods. The former are those cases where there is some interference of one person's actions on the well-being of others. This may be detrimental in that the individual's private pay-off is largely at the expense of pay-offs to others, or may be beneficial, in which case the private pay-off to the decision-maker fails to reflect the additional benefit a particular decision may confer on others. In both of these cases the nature of the interaction is, however, such that the spillover effect cannot be traded since if it were possible to so trade the externality would soon disappear; an equilibrium strategy involving all participants would be found. Public goods involve more extreme cases of divergence of the social from the private pay-off in that they represent those goods or activities in which no trade at all could take place without prior collusion or governmental intervention. The identification of the pure public good has proved a somewhat elusive goal since it is very difficult to find a good or service which displays the basic principles of inability to exclude by price and total non-rivalry between consumers (Peston, 1972). Nevertheless the basic concept of the public good as one where the trading game would fail to produce even a sub-optimal equilibrium remains a useful one.

The literature on these aspects of economic life is large and forms much of the basis of welfare economics and public economics. It is interesting from our point of view to note that even in the literature of non-spatial economics the examples of such effects have a predominantly spatial flavour in their concentration on questions of congestion and the effects of location, especially through the pollution question. These two cases, congestion and pollution, are particularly useful since they enable us to consider a further classification of types of externality and also because, although they do not relate exclusively to transport and location decisions respectively, they do enable us to develop these two aspects of spatial decision-making somewhat further.

Congestion-type externalities are generic to the whole question of transport choice although they characterise any situation where there is a demand function which is highly peaked temporally or spatially – relative inability to vary supply capacity in the short run and no possibility of storage from one period to the next; they can be seen, for example, to apply equally well to the question of competition over urban land uses. The basic characteristic of congestion is that it involves an external effect imposed by one user on another user and is hence typically a producer–producer or consumer–consumer conflict. Hence in the classic example of congestion on a single road each additional user imposes costs on all other users of that same road, although naturally in many instances each additional user cannot be individually identified as demand does not arise sequentially.

The nature of the analysis proceeds on the basis of the assumption that the marginal private costs of provision of a particular transport service are rising. This is particularly true in the road case, where for a private motorist time-costs will represent a high proportion of marginal costs. Additional users beyond a given volume of traffic cause the speed of other vehicles to be reduced and hence for a given journey the time taken increases. If we were to add the costs associated with comfort and convenience these would show a similar pattern, as indeed would traction costs as fuel consumption and general vehicle wear and tear increase. Note here that this rising marginal cost associated with increased *usage of a given transport service* contrasts with the general presumption of falling average costs for the *provision of transport services*, reflecting again the problem of fixity of capacity in both infrastructure and vehicles, the classic indivisibility problem.

However, if costs to the individual user are rising then the sum of costs to all users must be rising faster. This is because the additional cost incurred by each additional usage made accrues not only to that unit but to all users. If we assume for ease that all users face the same cost function it is easy to show that the marginal private cost is in fact equivalent to an average social cost and the marginal social cost is above the rising average social cost and rising faster (Walters, 1961).

This solution is illustrated graphically in Figure 5.1, which also demonstrates clearly that the appropriate modification to private costs necessary to bring about the optimal level of usage is given by the imposition of a unit tax of amount TV. Hence for the congestion case we have a clear-cut solution in terms of an optimal tax structure which makes all decision-makers perceive the true social costs of their actions and enables them to modify their behaviour accordingly. The tax structure thus effectively internalises the externality and decision-makers can act as if it did not exist – they achieve private optima and society reaches its best position. Furthermore, since investment decisions require an initially optimum allocation of resources, such a system also provides more robust criteria for identifying where additional capacity in the transport system is needed (Beesley and Walters, 1970).

There are, however, problems if we remove the assumption of a homogeneous market for the service in question where all users face the same cost function, since here an optimal tax structure is more difficult to identify and even more difficult to implement in practice. As we saw in Chapter 2, it is very difficult to identify a single transport market – many individuals with widely differing behavioural responses make up the total demand for a given transport service, such as an urban road.

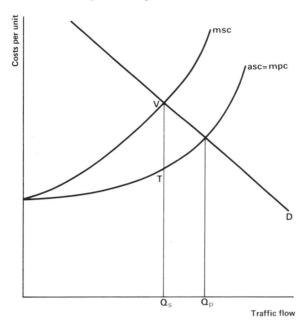

F IG. 5.1

These different groups will also face different marginal private costs. Whilst a situation such as this is found in many public-sector industries such as electricity supply and is often characterised by discriminatory pricing (output being fixed with reference to an aggregate demand function and total marginal costs and allocated to each sub-market by equating the relevant marginal costs, thus tending to increase prices for groups with inelastic demands and reducing prices for those with more elastic demands as in Figure 5.2), there are added difficulties in the transport case.

Firstly there is the implicit valuation problem. We have already referred to problems in evaluating such factors as time-savings for individuals. These problems are compounded when it is necessary to aggregate such values for groups of dissimilar people. Secondly, but following on from this, there is the distributional question. Partly this is the result of the problems of resolving the apparent conflicts between behavioural and resource values implicit in most valuations and considerations of equity. In the congestion case groups with inelastic demands, commuters and business travellers, who are forced to pay

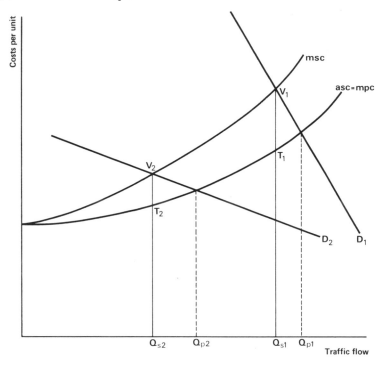

F IG. 5.2

relatively more of the congestion tax on the basis of Figure 5.2, are those with higher valuations of time and other factors. Hence the familiar arguments over subsidies to commuter-based urban railways arise – should those with higher behavioural and resource values of time, for example, be penalised? Partly it also involves the question of what should be done about the so-called transport-disadvantaged, those groups with poorer access to transport networks for either locational or economic reasons. Should transport networks be used as an instrument of more general social policy to alleviate poverty? Certainly physical access through transport networks is the most tangible aspect of the more general social inaccessibility to various facets of life which such groups face.

These more general issues obviously lie at the heart of the social aspects of our spatial economic problems and much greater weight needs to be placed on these both at the level of theoretical analysis and at the level of policy analysis than has so often been the case hitherto.

Simple and neat solutions to the congestion-type externality problem are not readily available in a spatial economy. The nature of demand and supply for the services in question precludes this.

Many of the same problems arise again in the case of pollution-type externalities, particularly the difficulties implicit in a world which does not consist of individuals all with equal property rights or economic power. The pollution type of externality is one which typically involves a user of a particular facility placing costs on or contributing benefits to a non-user of that facility, usually through infringements of general property rights in an environmental resource such as air, water, or peace and quiet. Hence a factory which pollutes the air or water imposes an externality on other types of producer, and on all other individuals benefiting from that common resource. A user of an international airport contributes to the noise which disturbs all those who live and work near the airport. It immediately becomes obvious that the distributional aspects of this are enormous since it is not now just the inequalities of income between road-users which affects our analysis, it is the inequalities of economic power between major industrial firms and individuals or between international airlines and individual residents.

The basic analysis of the problem is reminiscent of the congestion case in that it involves attempting to internalise the externality into the decision-maker's pay-off function. We assume that the externality in question is produced as part of an activity which faces diminishing returns to scale over the relevant range of output, i.e. the private net return to the producer is falling as line BQ_p in Figure 5.3. Beyond a certain output level, Q_o, there is a marginal external cost which is a rising function of output. We could conduct a parallel exercise for benefits with a marginal external benefit function which would fall as output rose with consequent opposite effects to those discussed here. The private optimal output for the producer is at Q_p, where marginal private benefits are zero, the socially optimal output is at Q_s, where the marginal private benefits are exactly equal to the marginal external costs. At levels of output below Q_s producers can compensate sufferers and still be better off, at levels of output above this the reverse is true. All that is necessary is the mechanism for securing output at level Q_s. This could be a tax on the producer of amount Q_sT or output controls to ensure that correct level of output.

Hence we have seen that whatever the nature of the externality it is possible to provide a theoretical means of internalising the effect such that a stable equilibrium can be achieved. The external effect can be

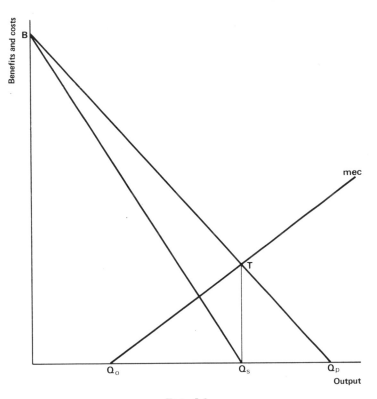

FIG. 5.3

introduced into the objective function of the sufferer (or beneficiary) such that instead of facing, for example, a utility function of the form

$$U_A = U_A(X_{1A}, X_{2A}, \ldots \ldots X_{nA}) \qquad (5.1)$$

where the subscript A refers to the person and the $X_1 \ldots \ldots X_n$ are quantities of goods, the effective form of the utility function in a two-person economy would be

$$U_A = U'_A(X_{1A}, X_{2A}, \ldots \ldots X_{nA}, X_{1B}) \qquad (5.2)$$

where activity 1 involves an external effect. In the congestion case this will be a reciprocal effect where X_{1A} appears in B's utility function, in the pollution case it is more likely to be a unidirectional effect. Internalisation and hence elimination of the external effect involves ensuring that the social cost of production of the external effect appears in the appropriate constraint for the causer(s) in the form of an effective shadow price. As noted above, this can either be done through imposition of an optimal tax or through physical controls which produce the same result.

The public goods case cannot be resolved so readily in theory, although we must also be careful not to minimise the practical difficulties in both calculating and implementing the optimal shadow price system in the externality case. The essence of the public goods case is that it is not possible to use even a modified market to effect allocation since the absence of a price-exclusion possibility makes it difficult to convey the correct market message. The only way of allocating the pure public good is by fixing an appropriate level of output by administrative means and financing this through general revenue taxation. There is, however, no way of knowing whether this level is in any sense economically optimal.

It has been argued, notably by Tiebout (1956), that a spatial economy does offer the best opportunity for establishing optimal levels of public good output. This occurs because most public goods, or near-public goods, are spatially limited. Beyond a certain distance range the generalised costs become such as to effectively exclude some from the benefits of such a good if it is produced at a single location. If several locations are used for production, as for example in the case where production is entrusted to local rather than central government authorities, then the producing authorities are free to vary production levels per capita and the corresponding levels of taxation to finance that production. In such a situation it is reasonable to suppose that authorities producing either too high a level of output, at a cost which renders the relative marginal utility to the individual consumers too low, or too low a level of output such that marginal utility is high relative to other goods may lose population to areas with authorities which are producing a more favourable combination. This idea of consumers voting with their feet is an appealing one and has found some empirical support in the area of educational provision in studies in the United States (Oates, 1969). However, the assumptions necessary to be able to argue that such a situation can produce optimal levels of production and consumption are very restrictive, and in economies where the freedom of local authorities to vary levels of provision outside a very limited range is itself limited it has only marginal empirical value. This approach does add a further dimension to the range of factors which must be considered important in locational studies, but the possibility of a stable and optimal equilibrium being attained must be seen as remote.

If equilibrium is not attainable in a given situation we must ask what will occur – can a sector be maintained in a state of disequilibrium, and if so what will be the effect of this on the behaviour of individual economic agents? We can only give a cursory look at this problem here but we shall return to this issue in more detail, after considering general equilibrium issues, in Chapter 7. There are basically two aspects to the disequilibrium problem. Firstly we can envisage a situation where the sector can adjust only slowly to its appropriate equilibrium, the situation that we have already seen will obtain frequently in sectors such as transport and building where the infrastructure is both lumpy and has long gestation periods from the recognition of need to the completion of construction. It may be considered to be undesirable on grounds such as those of equity to introduce measures to correct externalities, congestion taxes for example, if the decision has already been taken to increase capacity. The sector is therefore maintained in a state of short-run disequilibrium but the basic decisions taken within the sector with regard to longer-term demand and supply are not altered and in the long run equilibrium is achieved. There are costs to such a situation which it is necessary to account for in any appraisal exercise but it does not alter the basic structure of decision-making for the sector.

The second situation is, as we shall see in Chapter 7, a much more problematic one, but also of much greater interest and practical importance. This is where the disequilibrium which occurs at a particular moment of time alters expectations and preferences about future decisions, but alters these differentially for different participants in the trading game situation. Here equilibrium would be achieved only by accident. This situation contrasts with our earlier prisoners' dilemma-type problem because it is not possible to introduce a collusive element to secure correct knowledge of joint pay-offs since we are talking not about known outcomes but expectations of likely outcomes. Frequently any deviation from an expected value may invoke not the usual stabilising corrective action of well-behaved markets, but destabilising action of the type characterised by, for example, the explosive cobweb (van Doorn, 1975).

COLLUSION IN SPATIAL CHOICE

We turn in the final section of this chapter to consider the possibilities and effects of collusion within sectors of the spatial economy. As we have seen in earlier parts of this chapter there are likely to be two sorts of collusion which may occur. Firstly, there is the voluntary collusion between participants in the trading game to secure a higher aggregate pay-off. Secondly, there is the situation where a voluntary collusion does not come about but there could be a social benefit from some co-operation between certain parties, or conversely where collusion between any number of participants occurs at the expense of other participants and to what may be judged to be the expense of the aggregate social pay-off. In these circumstances there is a case for social control in the form of government intervention in the sector. Governments are in effect a formalisation of collusion between parties and of course reflect the difficulties in achieving a unanimous consensus such that the side-payments involved in the game (the means of sharing out the pay-off achieved from a coalition) become the matters of greatest importance; these are represented by voting in the case of governments.

The establishing of various forms of coalition between some or all of the various parties to trading games within the spatial economy can be as informal as the exchange of information, even indirectly through such media as trade papers or the general media of press and television, or involve a much more formal organisational structure. Much of this is little different from the sort of action traders would be expected to take in a non-spatial economy and hence need not concern us greatly here. One form of coalition which has received some attention in this context and is of particular relevance to the spatial economy is the concept of the club.

Clubs have been recognised as an important economic concept for some time. They represent the most obvious form of collusive partnership within a game conflict situation since they are essentially self-governing associations with specific objectives. Clubs can also be seen as lying at the heart of spatial economies, particularly in transport and urban matters. In some senses the growth and development of cities themselves represent the club, since cities are initially voluntary groupings of individuals for mutual benefit, defence and economic advancement. Similarly, in a historical context, transport can be seen to develop initially by the collective enterprise of groups with common interests. As we saw earlier the high infrastructural costs of transport tend to preclude private provision and uncertainty has often precluded purely speculative private-venture capital (with the notable exception of railway development in the early stages). However, following this argument also leads to another expectation, the volatility of club organisation. Once provided, infrastructure exists; and the rationale for the club declines unless it can preserve exclusive use of the infrastructure. Clubs, like all coalitions, are inherently unstable organisations subject to continual change through renegotiation and always likely to be undermined by defection.

SUMMARY

We have developed a number of themes in this chapter which concern the relationships between different decision-makers. The conflicts which are present can be seen as arising both within groups of similar decision-makers, consumers and producers, and between such groups. Our particular concern has been to consider whether such interaction in spatial markets results in the production of stable equilibria. Where markets do not converge readily on such an equilibrium the importance of strategy in decision-making becomes all-important.

The conclusion drawn is that in most cases the introduction of spatial considerations does disturb the possibility of achieving equilibrium and reduces the possibility of an easy resolution to conflict. However, it has also been seen that it is important to separate the purely informational problems of the spatial economy from those concerning the nature of production. It is not just the purely spatial sectors such as transport and housing which present problems of increasing returns to scale and indivisibilities. All production which concentrates in space must have increasing returns over the relevant range of output and the further analysis of this problem suggests that discontinuities may also be important.

These rather more basic microeconomic considerations of the spatial economy have often tended to be ignored in comparison to the more obvious externality conflicts which have dominated so much of urban economics in the past. This is not to deny that externality problems are the source of important social-benefit losses but it does raise the question of which ideal we should use for comparison. This theme forms the basis of much of Chapter 7 but before we can analyse this more fully we need to consider the interactions between sectors in addition to those interactions between decision-makers within sectors examined in this chapter.

GUIDE TO FURTHER READING

Theories of games and conflict start with the classic works of von Neumann and Morgenstern (1947), Luce and Raiffa (1957) and Rapoport (1961) but there are admirable reviews in the books by Weintraub (1975) and Bacharach (1976).

Useful introductions to supply characteristics, organisation and potential conflicts in transport are contained in Thomson (1974) and Gwilliam and Mackie (1975). A readable and more wide-ranging account is that of Schaeffer and Sclar (1975). Similar functions for the housing market are served by Whitehead (1974), Charles (1977) and Stafford (1977).

The best single source on the spatial organisation of markets is Greenhut and Ohta (1975) supplemented by various papers by Eaton and Lipsey which deal with a variety of aspects of spatial markets (1977, 1978). The classic views on spatial competition are those of Hotelling (1929), Smithies (1941) and Lerner and Singer (1939).

The theory of externalities is usefully reviewed in Bohm (1973) and Pearce (1976), and various practical applications can be found in Pearce (1978). The classic solution to the congestion problem is in Walters (1961), and its relation to investment criteria can be followed in Beesley and Walters (1970) and Gwilliam and Nash (1972). The main problem in determining optimal pricing is the usual second-best problem to which a possible solution is offered by Glaister and Lewis (1978). Some further conflicts over accessibility are highlighted in Hillman *et al.* (1973, 1976).

Optimal public goods provision in a spatial context is due to Tiebout (1956) and empirically tested by Oates (1969). A theory of clubs has been outlined by Buchanan (1965) and Pauly (1970) and introduced more explicitly into the question of urban growth and city size by Evans (1972).

REFERENCES

Bacharach, M. (1976), *Economics and the Theory of Games* (London: Macmillan).
Beesley, M. E., and Walters, A. A. (1970), 'Some problems in the evaluation of urban road investments', *Applied Economics*, 1, 241–60.
Bohm, P. (1973), *Social Efficiency* (London: Macmillan).

Buchanan, J. M. (1965), 'An economic theory of clubs', *Economica*, 32, 1–14.

Charles, S. (1977), *Housing Economics* (London: Macmillan).

Eaton, B. H., and Lipsey, R. G. (1977), 'The introduction of space into the neoclassical model of value theory', in M. J. Artis and A. R. Nobay (eds.), *Studies in Modern Economics* (Oxford: Basil Blackwell).

Eaton, B. H., and Lipsey, R. G. (1978), 'Freedom of entry and the existence of pure profit', *Economic Journal*, 88, 455–69.

Evans, A. W. (1972), 'The pure theory of city size in an industrial economy', *Urban Studies*, 9, 49–77.

Glaister, S., and Lewis, D. (1978), 'An integrated fares policy for transport in Greater London', *Journal of Public Economics*, 9, 341–55.

Greenhut, M. L. (1970), *A Theory of the Firm in Economic Space* (New York: Meredith).

Greenhut, M. L., and Ohta, H. (1975), *Theory of Spatial Pricing and Market Areas* (Durham, N. C.: Duke U. P.).

Gwilliam, K. M., and Mackie, P. J. (1975), *Economics and Transport Policy* (London: Allen & Unwin).

Gwilliam, K. M., and Nash, C. A. (1972), 'Evaluation of urban road improvements – a comment', *Applied Economics*, 4, 307–15.

Hillman, M., Henderson, I., and Whalley, A. (1973), *Personal Mobility and Transport Policy*, Broadsheet No. 542 (London: Political and Economic Planning).

Hillman, M., Henderson, I., and Whalley, A. (1976), *Transport Realities and Planning Policy*, Broadsheet No. 567 (London: Political and Economic Planning).

Hotelling, H. (1929), 'Stability in competition', *Economic Journal*, 39, 41–57.

Lerner, A. P., and Singer, H. W. (1939), 'Some notes on duopoly and spatial competition', *Journal of Political Economy*, 45, 145–86.

Luce, R. D., and Raiffa, H. (1957), *Games and Decisions* (New York: Wiley).

Oates, W. E. (1969), 'The effects of property taxes and local spending on property values; an empirical study of tax capitalization and the Tiebout hypothesis', *Journal of Political Economy*, 77, 957–71.

Pauly, M. V. (1970), 'Cores and clubs', *Public Choice*, 9, 53–65.

Pearce, D. W. (1976), *Environmental Economics* (London: Longman).

Pearce, D. W. (ed.) (1978), *The Valuation of Social Cost* (London: Allen & Unwin).

Peston, M. (1972), *Public Goods and the Public Sector* (London: Macmillan).

Pryke, R. W. S., and Dodgson, J. S. (1975), *The Rail Problem* (London: Martin Robertson).

Rapoport, A. (1961), *Fights, Games and Debates* (Ann Arbor: Michigan U.P.).

Schaeffer, K. H., and Sclar, E. (1975), *Access for All: Transportation and Urban Growth* (Harmondsworth: Penguin).

Smithies, A. (1941), 'Optimal location in spatial competition', *Journal of Political Economy*, 49, 423–39.

Stafford, D. C. (1977), *The Economics of Housing Policy* (London: Croom Helm).

Thomson, J. M. (1974), *Modern Transport Economics* (Harmondsworth: Penguin).

Tiebout, C. M. (1956), 'A pure theory of local expenditures', *Journal of Political Economy*, 64, 416–24.

van Doorn, J. (1975), *Disequilibrium Economics* (London: Macmillan).

von Neumann, J., and Morgenstern, O. (1947), *Theory of Games and Economic Behaviour* (Princeton, N. J.: Princeton U.P.).

Walters, A. A. (1961), 'The theory and measurement of private and social cost of highway congestion', *Econometrica*, 19, 676–99.

Weintraub, E. R. (1975), *Conflict and Co-operation in Economics* (London: Macmillan).

Whitehead, C. M. E. (1974), *The U.K. Housing Market: An Econometric Model* (Farnborough: Saxon House).

6 Towards General Equilibrium

Although we have discussed in some detail the interaction of economic decision from the point of view both of conflicts and coalitions our modelling of this has so far only been an extension of the basic single-sector decision models. We have seen both how other sectors' decisions act as exogenous influences on one sector's decisions and how the latter are modified by feedbacks generated endogenously in the former. We have not, however, made any attempt to add the various sectors together to obtain a picture of the workings of the entire spatial economy. General equilibrium modelling, the simultaneous achievement of equilibrium situations in all sectors of a given economy is, it must be made clear at the outset, both naïve and complex. It is naïve because of the simplifications which must obviously be made to render even the smallest economy a tractable problem. It is complex because of the number of relationships which exist in such an economy. However, general equilibrium is the obvious logical extension of the relationships we are considering, since it is only by considering an economy in general equilibrium that we can draw certain important inferences about its behaviour and the likely responses of the various economic agents within it. In this chapter we shall elaborate on the general nature of such an approach, in Chapter 7 we shall consider some further modelling developments and the drawbacks and limitations of the approach with indications of possible alternatives.

A·MODEL OF GENERAL EQUILIBRIUM

Equilibrium in a market involves finding a situation where there is no inducement for either party to a trading game to change his plans for a subsequent period except as a response to completely exogenous influences. It is therefore a situation of market clearing, implying that the traders are achieving the maximum pay-off possible under the existing constraints. An economist's interest in equilibrium is twofold. Firstly, we are interested in its existence, that is in the conditions which must obtain for the various trading parties to reach the equilibrium situation and in particular the vector of prices which is associated with it. Secondly, we are interested in whether the equilibrium is stable since it may be possible to find a set of conditions which would be consistent with equilibrium only to discover that there is no way that the economy can converge on the point: any slight deflection away from equilibrium then becomes cumulative.

Let us consider for the moment only a static equilibrium situation, one in which we are only interested in finding a single position for a single period and not in the behaviour of the economy through time. Such models of the spatial economy have concerned themselves with two basic tasks, firstly that of determining the allocation of a given land area between the alternative competing uses and secondly that of determining an optimal size of the given spatial economy, either in terms of physical (land area) size or, more commonly, of population.

The most basic of such models is concerned purely with the allocation of land to housing and transport. We start with individual utility functions expressed over consumption of goods (c) and space (s). Utility is maximised subject to a conventional money-budget constraint determined by income (y), the price of goods (p), rent at a particular location (r_i) and transport (commuting) costs at that location (t_i).

$$\max U = U(c, s) \tag{6.1}$$

subject to

$$y = pc + r_i s + t_i \tag{6.2}$$

In order to proceed further two simplifications are typically made. It is easier to treat c as a composite good and use it as a numeraire such that $p = 1$. The utility function is also given a specific form – the Cobb-Douglas is the most common since it is linear in the logarithms, but the more general constant elasticity of substitution model can be used.

Hence we can rewrite (6.1) and (6.2) as

$$\max U = \alpha \log c + (1 - \alpha) \log s \tag{6.3}$$

subject to

$$y = c + r_i s + t_i \tag{6.4}$$

which produces first-order conditions of the form

$$r_i s = \frac{\alpha c}{1 - \alpha} \tag{6.5}$$

and
$$r_i' s + t_i' = 0 \tag{6.6}$$

where r_i' and t_i' represent the first derivatives with respect to changes in i. Equation (6.6) is the well-established trade-off relationship that any increase in rent for a given site must be exactly equalled by a change in transport costs to preserve equilibrium. The critical price in the system is then the rent structure since once this is found the equilibrium transport costs will also be determined from (6.4) and (6.5).

$$y = \frac{(1 - \alpha)}{\alpha} r_i s + r_i s + t_i$$
$$\therefore \alpha(y - t_i) = r_i s \tag{6.7}$$

Using (6.6) we can derive a differential equation of the form

$$\frac{r_i'}{r_i} = \frac{1}{\alpha}\left(\frac{-t_i'}{y - t_i}\right) = \frac{1}{\alpha}\frac{d}{dr}\log(y - t_i) \tag{6.8}$$

from which the rent function

$$r_i = r_o\left(\frac{y - t_i}{y - t_o}\right)^{1/\alpha} \tag{6.9}$$

follows where the subscripts o refer to values at the centre of the city. Since $t_o = 0$ by assumption, (6.9) is more conveniently written as

$$r_i = r_o(1 - t_i/y)^{1/\alpha} = r_o w_i^{1/\alpha} \tag{6.10}$$

where w_i is the fraction of income left to a resident at i after allowing for commuting and hence from (6.7) we can derive an expression for the value of s at i as

$$s_i = \frac{\alpha y}{r_o} w_i^{1 - 1/\alpha} \tag{6.11}$$

Thus the key determinants of both rents and space allocated are total income, transport rates and the rents of central sites.

The rents of central sites can be determined by knowing the total degree of competition for available land in terms of the number of households. Assume a total of N households and that at any location i, represented by a ring of an assumed circular city of width di the proportion of land used for housing is $h_i(1 - h_i$ being used for transport). The supply of housing sites at location i (i.e. within the ring defined by inner radius i and outer radius $i + di$) is given by $2\pi ih_i di$. If $n_i di$ households seek sites of size s_i then for equilibrium in the housing market

$$s_i n_i di = 2\pi ih_i di \qquad (6.12)$$

and substituting for s_i from (6.11) gives

$$n_i = \frac{2\pi r_o ih_i w_i^{1/\alpha - 1}}{\alpha y} \qquad (6.13)$$

and since $N = \int_{i_o}^{i_b} n_i di$, where i_b is the radius of the city boundary,

$$N = \frac{2\pi r_o}{\alpha y} \int_{i_o}^{i_b} ih_i w_i^{1/\alpha - 1} di \qquad (6.14)$$

from which r_0 can be derived if h_i is known.

This model can be made more realistic by introducing a congestion function such that t_i depends not only on i but also on the ratio of number of residents at location i to available road space $(2\pi i(1 - h_i))$. In this way transport costs depend on population density which, through a relationship derived from (6.14), itself depends on transport costs.

At any location i the users of road space will be all those living at distances greater than i from the centre requiring to commute. If we call the total population living outside the ring of radius i, $N(i)$, we can write

$$N(i) = \int_i^{i_b} n_u du \qquad (6.15)$$

The aggregate road space available at i, it will be recalled, can be written as $2\pi i(1 - h_i)$. Thus the cost of commuting per person per unit distance at i will be given as

$$c_i = a\left(\frac{N(i)}{2\pi i(1 - h_i)}\right)^m \qquad (6.16)$$

and the total travel cost for a commuter from i

$$t_i = \frac{a}{(2\pi)^m} \int_{i_o}^i \left(\frac{N(u)}{u(1 - h_u)}\right)^m du \qquad (6.17)$$

This completes the circular dependence since location depends on t_i, hence $N(i)$ depends on t_i as a result of the decisions embodied in equation (6.13), but t_i itself depends on $N(i)$ through equation (6.17). The model is complete but extremely complex to solve analytically as are many of these models. Numerical solutions have therefore tended to dominate particular applications. It is worth noting in this context that some success has been achieved with the use of simplicial search algorithms for identifying equilibrium values in spatial models, although this technique is beyond the scope of this chapter.

The final stage is to consider variations in h_i such that it becomes a complete land use and transport model of the simple two-sector economy. Solow (1972) shows how, using an indirect utility function derived from (6.3), variations in h_i which lead to variations in r_o through (6.14) can be given a value in the utility function. An optimal h_i is one which generates a minimum r_o. Hence the model can be used to determine an optimal allocation of land to transport, although for feasible computation it will be necessary to assume that h_i is constant for all i.

This is a very naïve economy with all transport commuting, and all commuting to a single central point, but no production. The next stage is therefore to introduce a production sector which both produces goods for the residents to buy and constitutes a source of demand for the productive inputs which they own. Production takes place in the central area which is assumed to have a radius i_o such that its area $A = \pi i_o^2$. Assuming a Cobb-Douglas production function for the composite commodity using inputs of labour (E) and land we obtain gross output

$$Q = \delta E^\alpha A^\beta \qquad (6.18)$$

where α, β are parameters such that $0 < \alpha, \beta < 1, \alpha + \beta > 1$. The latter condition reflects increasing returns to scale which it is necessary to assume to allow for the urban area to exist at all. Costs of production other than labour involve the rent of the land and the rental of capital equipment, which it is assumed is employed in a fixed radio, δ, to land. Consumers receive a reward in terms of goods but part of their income must also be spent on rent of land. If we assume that land rents paid to landlords are independent of use then we can aggregate all rental payments within a city of total radius i_b as $\pi r i_b^2$ where r is the average rent per unit. Net production available for consumption is therefore given by $Q - \pi r i_b^2 - \delta \pi i_o^2$.

On the factor supply side we are interested particularly in the labour input. Assuming a homogeneous labour force such that man-hours can be aggregated and that all individuals have an equal commitment of time to necessary domestic and leisure activities total labour available will be given by available man-hours less commuting time. If the population of the area is N and the hours available per person net of committed time are H then we can write

$$E = NH - \int_{i_o}^{i_b} [T_i - N_i' di]$$ (6.19)

where $-N'_i di$ is the population of the ring of inner radius i and outer radius $(i + di)$ and T_i is the travel cost function

$$T_i = t_i + \tau [N_i/(1 - h_i)2\pi i di]^\kappa$$ (6.20)

where t_i is the pure distance cost of travel, τ and κ are the parameters of the congestion effect.

Thus we have an internally consistent model which determines labour inputs as a function of time and travel with congestion, production as a function of labour and land inputs and an objective function which depends on the consumption goods produced by the productive process. The model is only soluble, however, if certain values are fixed exogenously, since otherwise it will produce a variety of possible sets of values. A range of possible initial values could be used but there are two particularly interesting approaches referred to by Richardson (1977) as the closed and open model. The former takes a purely internal view of the city by fixing its population exogenously and using the model structure just to achieve internal allocation. The latter attempts to determine not just optimum internal allocation but also optimal size by making population endogenous and fixing the utility level on the grounds that this would be a national rather than an urban phenomenon. This approach has the advantage that it does place urban areas within the context of a wider situation and opens the way to consideration of an optimum geography (Mirrlees, 1972).

A further question which optimisation in a general equilibrium framework requires us to tackle is the relationship between individual utility and the social welfare function. Implicit in the simplest models of the urban economy of which that outlined above is an example is a city of identical consumers whose preferences can be aggregated additively into the total welfare function of the city. Maximising the latter implies maximising all the former. There are a number of problems with this approach, not the least of which is that a structure based on this additive assumption does not necessarily produce an equal distribution of benefits.

Whilst this unequal treatment of identical people is a problem, a much more serious one is the initial assumption of identical consumers. A city which consisted of identical individuals, i.e. those with equal initial resources and identical preference structures would not only be rather uninteresting but would appear to be economically non-viable. Apart from difficulties with various production relationships it is difficult to conceive how any form of spatial organisation would develop apart from the two extremes of total point-concentration (which is impossible) or total dispersion (which was assumed away by concentration of production at a point). It would seem that a reasonably recognisable city requires both inequality and variations in preferences for its existence.

Given this, there must be some concept of optimum inequality, i.e. the degree of inequality necessary to produce the social optimum. This inequality has been examined by various authors including Riley (1973), Stern (1973) and Dixit (1973) in a number of different ways. Riley, for example, uses a product rule to define the social welfare function, Dixit uses a constant elasticity function in which a parameter measures the degree of inequality; in the limit, as the parameter goes to infinity, this is equivalent to the well-known criterion of Rawls (1971). One point emerging clearly from these various approaches is that locational preferences are important additional arguments to the individual's utility function. This is usually incorporated as a measure of distance to the workplace as a proxy for a more general location indicator. There remain certain difficulties with this variable, however. Mirrlees's model noted earlier does incorporate this distance factor but the functional form used for the total welfare of the city implies that both the other arguments, in consumption and space, are functions of location such that all persons in each distance-band have identical patterns of consumption and land use. Furthermore it is not clear *a priori* whether utility for the individual should be a decreasing or increasing function of distance from the workplace. The simple model suggests that a decreasing function is reasonable and this assumption leads naturally to the downward-sloping rent function described above. Once external factors such as environmental quality are introduced then this assumption is less clear.

The real problem is, however, that of the nature of location itself, its individuality and exclusivity, which renders it inappropriate for analysis by the economist's conventional tools of smooth convex functions. Unlike normal consumption goods or space an individual must consume a fixed 'amount of location' i.e. a given transport input when once the decision has been taken. Moreover, only one location can be consumed at once – once chosen, a given location excludes all others. Such a situation would seem to be appropriate for a mathematical programming solution since this enables us to escape from the constraints imposed on functional form by the integral calculus basis typical of the equilibrium modelling described so far. The main protagonist of this approach has been Mills (1972) although a more specific model of residential structure was developed much earlier by Herbert and Stevens (1960).

The Mills model has a number of attractive features. Space is represented as a grid pattern such that location can be made more precise than with the concentric circle model and also non-symmetrical cities can be derived. Each square of the grid can also be developed at different densities and building heights, thus allowing for a critical capital–land substitution in the technology. The model can incorporate more easily a variety of goods with differing production technologies and an exchange of exported goods for imported factors. The model is written as a cost-minimisation exercise for the city as a whole, subject to a series of constraints, most of which are the logical resource or non-negativity relationships. This model is particularly useful because it can produce a range of city structures from a decentralised city where employment equals housing potential in each square to the completely centralised city where employment is concentrated in the central squares and housing in the peripheral ones. We shall develop this model in a little more detail and make a fuller assessment in the next chapter, but we must now return to our primary interest, that of the implications of the general equilibrium model for our analysis of spatial behaviour.

As stated at the outset the technical aspects of the general equilibrium are concerned with existence and stability. Assuming that these conditions are fulfilled by a model, such as those considered above, what does this tell us about the economy and the behaviour of the individual decision-takers within it? First of all it means that for every trading game, whether of two or more people, there exists a solution value and that there is no endogenous inducement to individuals to change their plans. The implications of this we have already discussed in Chapter 5. Secondly, since the equilibrium is stable there is no tendency for an exogenous change to wreak havoc with such solutions – the system can adjust to a new set of solution values. However, being able to identify such solutions does not necessarily tell us what the final structure of the economy will be since there will typically be a range of acceptable solutions until some external reference-point is introduced.

Typically this external reference is a criterion of social optimality. The application of the Pareto criterion that an optimum occurs where no single individual economic agent can be made better off without simultaneously causing another to be made worse off, is an example of this. General equilibrium models of a non-spatial nature can proceed from this to demonstrate that under conditions of perfect competition, with many traders and free entry and exit, a unique solution will emerge consistent with the Pareto criterion. Spatial models are not so easy since the assumption of spatial differentiations and its natural concomitant of returns to scale destroy this neat and precise solution. Nevertheless it is possible to obtain equilibrium solutions to spatial models quite easily, although they may lack the neat elegance of the non-spatial perfectly competitive world. For the solution to be socially optimal it will normally be necessary to impose constraints from outside and, in the real world, to use the various policy variables available to control the economy to that optimum.

The general equilibrium model thus serves as a yardstick, an ideal solution to which the economy should be guided as a prerequisite for the achievement of a socially optimal situation. Let us turn in the remainder of this chapter to a consideration of the characteristics of each of the main sectors of the local economy when this optimal state exists.

THE TRANSPORT SECTOR IN EQUILIBRIUM

It will have become clear from the model outlined above that the treatment of the transport sector is very cursory. The primary purpose of the model is to allocate land to transport use according to the requirements of the spatial distribution of other land uses, but allowing for the feedback present in the fact that the allocation to transport affects transport costs and hence the optimal locations of these other activities. In doing so it has assumed a homogeneous uni-modal transport service with known cost functions for all users and a known common response by all users to variations in the various elements of those costs. This is not a very useful model to investigate the transport sector in any detail but let us see what it can tell us and how certain more realistic modifications may change matters.

First of all the model has assumed a known, fixed transport technology which determines exogenously traction costs per mile (t_i in equation (6.20)) and the congestion effects (τ and κ in (6.20)). The only endogeneity is in terms of the level of usage. The transport infrastructure is assumed given, and the supply of transport services is totally demand-responsive up to capacity. As congestion effects get stronger in a zone, using land for transport becomes more worth while and hence capacity is increased at the expense of other land uses. The adjustment to equilibrium is therefore purely in terms of the allocation of land to transport and the implicit, congestion-cost-determined, total price.

Any exogenous technical progress in transport which results either in lower traction costs or an effective increase in transport capacity per unit of land input will cause a reduction in T_i'. The basic effect of this is through equation (6.19) on the supply of labour and hence the optimal population which the area can support. If population is regarded as fixed then the city can simply become smaller. This, however, is based on the assumption that the transport network is completely regular. In practice this is unlikely and improvements tend to be concentrated on particular links. The sort of improvement in mind here is the minor change in network characteristics such as junction improvements or traffic-control techniques on the roads, the introduction of automatic signalling or train control on rail systems, or improvements in fare collection systems which reduce stop times for buses.

If such changes in the transport cost function operated differentially on zones at the same distance from the centre then the effect of this would be to change the optimal distribution of the population. The suburbanising effects of various transport improvements, electric street tramways, underground railways, rapid transit systems and urban motorways are well established both in terms of historical and theoretical models.

The equilibrium allocation of land to transport obtained from this model is of course that resulting from free competition and is not therefore necessarily an optimal allocation. We know that, in general, under conditions of congestion the social cost will be greater than private cost at the margin and this will induce over-use of a given transport capacity. If some form of optimal congestion tax is introduced this has the effect of increasing perceived transport costs and reducing the amount of transport desired. The *optimal* allocation of land to transport is therefore in general less than the competitive allocation at each location and the city is accordingly either more compact, if of a fixed population, or larger in population terms, if of a fixed area.

Critical to the efficiency of the transport sector and hence the optimal devotion of resources to it is the structure of the transport network. The problem with the equilibrium model of an urban area is that it is essentially just a generalisation of a one-dimensional linear location model to an areal situation. Whilst it is logical to generalise land usage and production by simple integration in a circular city, transport is different since its allocation of land is not represented in the one-dimensional case and the implication is carried that any point is a given ring of internal radius i and width di has an identical level of transport service. This may be a reasonable assumption *on average*, or if points are construed as having a spatial dimension of their own, but transport is obviously more efficient, as we saw in Chapter 5, if it is concentrated to enjoy the considerable scale economies present (especially in the provision of infrastructure). Transport is not infinitely variable over space but must be concentrated in discrete forms. The question is what form should this be?

The equilibrium model cannot help here, it simply considers the level of traffic generated from within and beyond each zone and aims to create sufficient capacity to cope with this centre-bound traffic – the capacity along all radial segments would be identical. Optimising a network so as to minimise the total allocation of land to transport in the entire urban area consistent with the requirements of the various demanders of transport and the costs of operation would lead to rather different results. There are thus three interrelating components of an optimising model for a network. First of all different shapes of network affect user costs both through distance and hence normal traction costs and through likely levels of congestion. Secondly, different networks have differing operating potential requiring differing forms of traffic control and so forth. Thirdly, the structure of the network can have important effects on the total land requirements given the scale economies possible in infrastructure provision such that a coarse high-density network can be more economical than a finer lower-density one. Any one of these could be selected as an objective with the other two as constraints and at least the land use and user cost objectives would be consistent with the remainder of the general equilibrium model which of course does not have a transport-operating sector.

Modifications to the transport sector of the model to take some account of these points could yield a useful extension to the model, both in terms of greater realism for the sector itself and in terms of allowing for the development of uneven cities which are nevertheless in equilibrium. Progress in this direction would also open the possibility of producing transport networks which were not only irregular but also hierarchical, involving in effect various grades of network coarseness and density superimposed on one another and linked. Once this possibility of varying the production technology is introduced it becomes simpler to consider an equilibrium model with different modes. Again the result of this will be to produce an important distinction between the competitive equilibrium and a situation involving the optimal allocation of resources to the various modes of transport.

One final consideration is what happens when the central area of the city is not a spaceless point at which all employment is located. Here transport within the central area as well as to it is relevant, although this of course serves a distribution rather than a trunk-haul function. The not surprising effect of incorporating such a feature in the model is that the greatest proportional devotion of land to transport is still at the edge of the central area and this declines towards the centre of that central area as well as towards the outer areas of the city, a pattern characteristic of real cities.

We have seen in the above extensions that it is quite feasible to incorporate a number of more realistic aspects of the transport sector into a general equilibrium framework and consider the effects on relative land use. However, it must still be noted that little consideration has been given to a genuine feedback from either residential or production sectors on the nature of transport other than its total quantity in an exogeneously fixed coefficients technology.

THE RESIDENTIAL SECTOR IN EQUILIBRIUM

The residential sector has formed the core of most general equilibrium models of urban areas. The problems of urban areas have typically been viewed as essentially social problems (such as urban decay, ghetto formation, crime, education, social services) which have an economic focus in the twin problems of housing and transport (or usually, more narrowly, just congestion). Interest has concentrated first of all in demonstrating that land-rent gradients will be typically negative with distance from the central area, and that starting with a community of identical individuals only in very special circumstances will equilibrium not have a bias to inequalities developing. Starting with initial inequalities, it becomes easy to see how problems develop with higher-income groups typically dominating peripheral developments, trading off the lower land-rents for increased space. Lower-income groups are forced into high-land-rent areas where they can only economise by reducing their demands for space.

The behaviour of the residential sector is essentially the same as that of the transport sector, since again an implicitly fixed coefficients technology for the supply of residential space is assumed. Variations in that technology would lead to a re-shuffling of land uses by affecting one of the fixed points necessary to establish the rent gradient. This will usually be the opportunity-cost rent at the city boundary, fixed by reference to its 'agricultural value'.

Just as the transport sector is a naïve one so is the typical residential sector. It is not a model of a housing sector since it involves no concept of either production or demand for anything but space. Richardson has characterised it most succinctly as residents being 'given tents by a relief organisation and they pitch them at the site size (and location) that maximises their utility' (Richardson, 1977). To turn the simple residential sector into a full housing market is, however, a move of some complexity · for three basic reasons, production, irreversibility and demand.

There is no intrinsic difficulty in introducing a housing production function. If we assume a fixed capital–land relationship for the moment, as in the production sector of equation (6.18), we can write housing production in a Cobb-Douglas formulation with increasing returns to scale as

$$H_i = \varepsilon E_i^\kappa A_i^\lambda \tag{6.21}$$

where E_i and A_i are labour and land requirements respectively, at location i, ε, κ, λ are constants, $0 < \kappa, \lambda < 1$; $\kappa + \lambda > 1$. Equilibrium in the housing market requires us to make a further assumption about housing demand. The simplest assumption is that each household requires one housing unit, a household consisting of a single worker, such that equilibrium requires us only to equate housing supply with resident workers at each location.

However, there are already a number of problems. The production of housing at location i requires labour such that unless the residents at i provide their own housing this interferes with the assumption that all employment is in the central area: we have non-radial commuting and a large part of the model crumbles. Production of housing is, of course, subject to considerable lags, which may lead to adjustment difficulties, and in reality there is likely to be a large array of possible capital/land ratios relevant, requiring more explicit consideration of a capital market. Housing is also typically provided speculatively by developers such that it is necessary for them to anticipate demand and develop housing of a particular type at a particular location prior to the realisation of that demand.

A major problem in considering equilibrium in the housing market is the absence of costless reversibility of investment decisions. Housing has both a long gestation period and a long life. Changes in other factors in the equilibrium model which induce a change in housing demand at a particular location, either quantitatively because of a change in population distribution or qualitatively, cannot easily be met if all land in that zone is already built upon. Thus even with the assumption of an infinitely variable factor ratio in production there will be a troublesome fixity not only in the type of housing actually available but also in quantity and plot size. Studies of real housing markets have suggested that new production is typically only equivalent to some $1\frac{1}{2}$ to 2 per cent of total housing stock in each year (Whitehead, 1974).

Possibly the greatest difficulty is in the introduction of housing demand. If housing is not of the refugee tent type and if housing developers are able to vary the quality of the housing produced, which seems likely if plot sizes and densities are variable, then the unit price of housing is likely to vary from a constant relationship to land rents. In such circumstances it will be necessary to introduce housing as a further element in the consumers' utility functions. Empirical studies of housing markets have encountered considerable difficulty in defining adequate measures of housing consumption. Obviously housing consists of a complex bundle of characteristics which can receive varying preferences and weights in different consumers' choice decisions. Whilst it may be possible to assess the relative importance of rooms, age, noise, environment and so forth in detailed studies of small housing markets, such an approach is not feasible in this general model of the urban area. Muth (1969) proposed the simple solution of using house values to express relative measures of housing supply in comparison with an arbitrarily chosen standard unit of housing. This method is crude but has certain merits of simplicity. It does depend, however, on a certain constancy in the determination of house prices.

The unit price of housing in a particular location will, in equilibrium, depend on a number of factors. Many of the models have attempted to ignore the variation in demand price which could be attributed to house quality and use just a location price, related as usual to transport costs. Supply price in a simple production model of the form of (6.21) can be shown to depend on location rent and the productivity of labour (or its usage in competitive equilibrium), each weighted by its appropriate factor share of λ and κ. In a more complex model, with a capital input as well, the implicit rental on that capital would also be a determinant. Hence changes in productivity in other sectors, notably the production sector, would have important effects on the price of housing and hence equilibrium in the residential sector. There is a natural circularity, however, in that land rents will depend not only on an arbitrary use of that land but also on the price of the housing placed upon it, since a developer will be prepared to bid a rent according to the value of the proposed development in terms of either the rental for use of building space or its capitalised value on resale.

The discussion above has illustrated the problems likely to be encountered when an explicit housing market is introduced albeit still in an exceedingly simple city. Once again, as with the transport sector, the omission of the production side of housing, and particularly here consumer preferences for different types of housing, is seen to ignore some important induced responses which could have an important effect on overall equilibrium.

Further complexities must remain unexplored. When developers have the choice between housing and other competing interests where employment is not centralised or when we consider the various possible external effects, the equilibrium position will change. The question of divergence between the competitive equilibrium and an optimal one arises again. It is interesting to note that many general equilibrium structures with housing sectors attempt to optimise a mainly production-based model, ignoring consumer preferences and potential inequalities. A final issue which we have touched on previously in the partial equilibrium context is the role of planning controls and land use zoning in restricting genuine free competition. This may be argued for on the grounds of correcting sub-optimalities in the competitive solution but is generally a crude measure which tends to fossilise the land-use map and accentuate the irreversibilities discussed above.

THE PRODUCTION SECTOR IN EQUILIBRIUM

The production sector is the vital sector of the whole model since it is this which produces the income to support the remainder of the city and the goods which satisfy consumer demand. Without a production sector a city is meaningless; and moreover, without a production sector which produces a surplus through increasing returns, the city is not viable. Part of this surplus is necessary to support the spatial structure through transport, the remainder tends to accrue in the rents to landowners. It is the former part which is critical, since if the returns to scale obtained by concentrating production are insufficient to support the transport system then necessary to move dispersed factors to the production point, and finished goods to the dispersed consumers, production would itself be better dispersed.

This is satisfactory as a starting-point but the surplus from the production sector of a real city which produces more than the single composite commodity comes not only from the internal scale economies implicit in the production function but also most significantly from external economies typically referred to as agglomeration economies. It is these agglomeration economies which provide the rationale for large multi-function cities. However they also lead to concentration of plants in the same industry in a single area against the normal tenet of simple spatial production theory, which predicts the growth of spatial monopolies. This simple approach assumes spatially invariant production costs such that a new entrant will always find it worth while to locate at a new site since although his factory door mill price will be no lower than existing firms' his delivered price will be lower for some of the market (assuming some dispersion of consumers). The effect of agglomeration economies is to give existing locations such favoured mill prices that no advantage on delivered prices can be obtained at any other location.

Once we start examining spatial market structures as part of the equilibrium model of the city it becomes obvious that we cannot consider the system as an isolated state. Agglomeration as the basis of city size and growth depends on not just a hinterland which acts as a perfectly elastic supplier of resources, typically labour, and an export market for the output of the production sector but also implies the existence of competing centres. The competition of these centres is both for resources and for markets. Agglomeration economies of the type discussed above which lead to concentration also imply specialisation of types of production and this in turn implies trade between cities. Hence, just as with countries or regions, the balance of trade is seen to be a critical determinant of city welfare and growth. Competition for resources, however, is more likely to prove to be a constraint on growth since these resources will normally need to be imported from the hinterland either in kind (labour, raw materials, etc.) or in terms of the surplus from hinterland production.

The critical relationship between trade and growth and welfare for small economic areas has long been recognised in terms of export base theories of city size and growth. These make the useful distinction between those productive activities which are surplus-producing and depend on a healthy demand from other areas and those which either serve the base as secondary productive activities or simply serve the community. The latter are the various urban infrastructure and service activities whose whole reason for existence is the concentration of primary activities. Recognition of this link provides a useful connection for us between the microeconomic concerns of individual agents in the spatial economy and the wider macroeconomic factors of total product and growth. It is easy to see that since the base sector is the income-generating sector it is necessary to effect increases in the base in order to support any planned increases in non-base activities.

Whilst the general equilibrium model can thus fit conveniently into the macroeconomic framework it leaves one important issue unresolved. So far we have maintained the assumption that all production is concentrated in an undefined central area. Production, and hence the city, can grow to an optimal size but this does not produce conflicts between the production and other sectors over land use. The central area is not fixed, it is actually spaceless since it appears to be infinitely variable without affecting the rest of the city – hence the rather appropriate concept of the hollow centre or 'doughnut' city used by several authors. Some attempts have been made, notably that by Livesey (1973), to examine the effects of land-use conflicts at the edge of the central area on both land rents and the devotion of land to transport. We have already noted the likely results of this in terms of peak land rents and the greatest devotion of land to transport occurring at the central area boundary. These are essentially static models, however, a much more interesting and practically relevant problem being the extent to which conflicts between production and other sectors over the use of land lead to constraints on city growth and welfare or to induced changes in the production sector to increase efficiency, particularly efficiency in the use of land.

Equilibrium in the production sector in the static model is thus seen to be of little interest, since the role of the production sector is essentially that of providing the dynamic impetus to city development. It is only when this has been considered that we can hope to introduce a discussion of the role of factor markets and particularly that of the urban labour market.

DYNAMICS IN THE GENERAL EQUILIBRIUM MODEL

Dynamic models of general equilibrium in local economies present enormous problems to the solution of which only faltering steps have been made. Essentially we are faced with a situation where we can make either spatial or temporal extensions to a static model of equilibrium, but to consider both dimensions simultaneously is beyond the scope of not only this book but also most current researchers. The reason for this is easy to see; the introduction of space has meant, first of all, the introduction of two new sectors, land and transport, and secondly the need to describe all activities by their locations. To introduce a time-dimension means that on top of this we must also consider the distribution of activities through time as well as space.

Not surprisingly those attempts at dynamics which have been made employ radical simplifications but they can nevertheless throw interesting insights on to behaviour. This is important for our purposes since the relative fixity of locations compared with other economic decisions implies that individuals and firms must take fairly long-run views; similar considerations must apply to transport infrastructure investment decisions. Furthermore, we also know that considerable speculation takes place in spatial markets, which can only be considered in a temporal context.

One approach has been to abstract from the spatial question and consider the effect of dynamics on particular sectors. The relationship between the housing market and urban growth has been explored by Evans (1975) and Muth (1976). Muth's model has two alternatives, assuming durability and non-durability of the stock. The durable model is akin to a vintage capital model. The main emphasis is on a comparison of results from these two assumptions. Durability implies higher population densities and lower land rents than non-durability, although these results depend not on a deterministic solution but a simulation with assumed initial parameter values and constant growth-rates of rents, incomes, land area and population. Evans' results differ from these in a rather different model but one also based on housing vintages. Evans does not include income changes; and rents in his model grow faster than does population, leading to higher rather than the lower rents of Muth's model. Again initial parameter values are critical.

Although these models are crude and have rather uncertain results they do show that assumptions of non-durability in just one sector do produce different results for key variables such as rent and density. It is easy to see that this can have important implications for all the variables in the simple equilibrium model.

Another non-spatial model of a dynamic urban area, related this time to the transport sector, is that of Glaister (1976). Glaister's concern was to show the effects of different transport pricing policies on the nature of urban growth when congestion is present. The potential growth pattern of the city in terms of population is based on the very naive assumption of a logistic curve which is modified by commuting transport costs. The money prices of the two available transport modes form the policy variables and various combinations of policy are available – constant prices, average cost prices, and marginal social cost prices. Efficiency is measured in terms of the benefits and costs to the marginal city resident.

Again the model can only be used to simulate results from initial values of the various parameters but it demonstrates clearly that variations in transport pricing can lead both to different rates of urban growth and long-run equilibrium city sizes and also to very different overall valuations. The most efficient pricing policy, which produces a larger city faster and at lower total social cost, appears not surprisingly as one based on marginal social costs although variations on this, including a car ban or a second-best pricing for buses, charging below bus marginal social costs by an amount reflecting car marginal social costs and the cross-elasticities of demand, can produce results fairly close to this optimum.

Some attempts have been made to consider both space and time simultaneously by avoiding continuous functions in one or both dimensions to overcome the problem of simultaneous integration. This leads us somewhat beyond the scope of this chapter into the realms of the next, but two models which retain continuous variables for the spatial dimension and simply introduce discrete time are worth mentioning.

Pines (1976) has developed a model to consider staged development planning in a city with inner and outer residential areas developed sequentially with no reversibility possible. The conclusions are again somewhat tentative but, as may be expected, imply that non-continuous growth and development may be optimal. Cities may grow irregularly and demonstrate irregular density gradients quite consistently with optimisation. The evidence of the model, however, is that these results are associated more strongly with the lack of reversibility and not just the introduction of time; and this would appear to be the crucial factor in such models.

The second approach is that of Anas (1976) which uses a two-period model, assumes myopic behaviour and new housing construction only on the periphery of the city but allows for abandonment, conversion and replacement of existing housing stock. The basic conclusion is again of non-regularity in rent gradients even to the extent of negative rents in inner areas which lead to abandonment. The working of the model is, however, constrained by the need to attain a temporary equilibrium period by period, this being defined very restrictively as equalising utilities over the whole city, a point we shall return to in the following chapter. The model does carry the interesting implication that sub-urbanisation may occur in the short run because of fringe discontinuities in the rent structure but on approaching its long-run equilibrium size a restructuring occurs. This is partly due to the assumed myopia and lack of speculation which could reduce these discontinuities but nevertheless represents another step towards producing less regular and possibly more realistic model cities.

SPATIAL GENERAL EQUILIBRIUM – A SUMMARY

General equilibrium involves the putting together of the various sectoral equilibria discussed previously and allowing for interactions between these to take place. The purpose of constructing such models is twofold; to understand something of the structure of the urban system and how it develops, and to be able to trace the effects of specific changes in particular variables throughout the system, especially where policy variables are concerned. The essence of models is to simplify and thus it is not a valid criticism of these models just to suggest that they represent an oversimplification. We need to show rather that they misrepresent certain key features of the system such that they produce misleading results.

Much of the obvious criticism centres around the difficulties associated with the simplifying assumptions of regular, circular, monocentric urban areas with homogeneous populations, single-commodity production sectors, one mode of transport used for only one purpose, and a uniform residential sector. Theoretical cities, it has been noted before, are not just puritanical but exceedingly dull. However, all of these assumptions are justifiable initial simplifications. We have discussed in more detail first of all the nature of the equilibrium state of the basic model and subsequently the effects of relaxing the strictness of various assumptions sector by sector. This latter step we have handled purely qualitatively however, since the complexities of the ensuing model would occupy more space than is justified by the new results they would produce.

The simple basic monocentric city is typified by the negative rent gradient and the negative density gradient. It also tends to produce inequality. The various modifications to assumptions do not fundamentally alter this pattern, they introduce irregularities into the various gradients, change optimal city size in terms of both population and area and generate different patterns of inequality. These changes are essentially matters of degree rather than of substance, although we have noted, somewhat critically at times, how they can produce cities which look substantially different from the prototype.

The real problems began to become apparent when we introduced the question of dynamics, how the city moves towards the identified long-run equilibrium. Two principal difficulties begin to appear. Firstly, in attempting to handle both space and time simultaneously we are forced to abandon assumptions of continuity and consider discrete functions. Once continuity is abandoned, even in just one dimension, more substantial irregularities in city structure appear which begin to be less compatible with the simple model. Secondly we need to consider carefully the whole question of equilibrium. Whilst it is both useful and necessary to retain the equilibrium concept in the long-run static model, since it provides a consistent and rational basis for comparing actual with optimal situations, a dynamic model based on a sequence of short-run temporary equilibria is more questionable. This does not involve a comparison of potential and ideal outcomes but instead represents the path via which the system moves towards that ultimate goal. In what sense can the urban economy be held to move into equilibrium period by period?

Both of these questions raise considerable issues beyond general equilibrium which are crucial to the structure of both any complete model of the urban system and a model of any part of that system. It is these further issues to which we turn in the following chapter.

GUIDE TO FURTHER READING

Basic introductions to the concept of general equilibrium in a non-spatial economy are Weintraub (1974) and Allingham (1975). The main developments in spatially extended models can be traced in Solow (1972, 1973), Mirrlees (1972) and Dixit (1973); these and many other models are reviewed in Richardson (1977). An interesting further development is the use of search algorithms to derive equilibrium solutions, first presented for a spatial model by MacKinnon (1974).

Previous models of land use and the spatial structure of cities date from the work of Haig (1926), Burgess (1925), and Hoyt (1939). The effects of transport on the shape and form of cities have been discussed by Meyer, Kain and Wohl (1966) and Schaeffer and Sclar (1975), and there is evidence for the changes brought about by railways in Kellett (1969), street tramways in Warner (1962), subway systems in Davies (1976) and motorways in Thomson (1969, 1977), amongst many others.

The spatial structure of residential markets is well reviewed and analysed in Evans (1973), but the *tour de force* in this area is the classic work of Muth (1969).

Dixit (1973) provides a good introduction to the production sector in space although the production sector is itself spaceless in this and many other models. The question of giving dimension to the central business district of cities has been principally tackled by Livesey (1973).

Export base theories serve as a useful introduction to dynamic aspects of local economies, and are well reviewed in Richardson (1978).

Muth (1976) and Evans (1975) have attempted to introduce time into their models. The rather differing approaches of Glaister (1976), Pines (1976) and Anas (1976) are also worthy of further study.

REFERENCES

Allingham, M. (1975), *General Equilibrium* (London: Macmillan).

Anas, A. (1976), 'Short run dynamics in the spatial housing market', in G. J. Papageorgiou (ed.), *Mathematical Land Use Theory* (Lexington, Mass.: D. C. Heath).

Burgess, E. W. (1925), 'The growth of a city', in R. E. Park, E. W. Burgess and R. D. Mackenzie, (eds), *The City* (Chicago: Chicago U.P.).

Davies, G. W. (1976), 'The effect of a subway on the spatial distribution of population', *Journal of Transport Economics and Policy*, 10, 126–36.

Dixit, A. (1973), 'The optimum factory town', *Bell Journal of Economics and Management Science*, 4, 637–51.

Evans, A. W. (1973), *The Economics of Residential Location* (London: Macmillan).

Evans, A. W. (1975), 'Rents and housing in a theory of urban growth', *Journal of Regional Science*, 15, 113–25.

Glaister, S. (1976), 'Transport pricing policies and efficient urban growth', *Journal of Public Economics*, 5, 103–17.

Haig, R. M. (1926), 'Towards an understanding of the metropolis', *Quarterly Journal of Economics*, 40, 197–208.

Herbert, J. D., and Stevens, B. H. (1960), 'A model of the distribution of residential activity in urban areas', *Journal of Regional Science*, 2, 21–36.

Hoyt, H. (1939), *Structure and Growth of Residential Neighbourhoods in American Cities* (Washington D.C.: Federal Housing Administration).

Kellett, J. R. (1969), *The Impact of Railways on Victorian Cities* (London: Routledge & Kegan Paul).

Livesey, D. A. (1973), 'Optimum city size: a minimum congestion cost approach', *Journal of Economic Theory*, 6, 144–61.

MacKinnon, J. (1974), 'Urban general equilibrium models and simplicial search algorithms', *Journal of Urban Economics*, 1, 161–83.

Meyer, J. R., Kain, J. F., and Wohl, M. (1966), *The Urban Transportation Problem* (Cambridge, Mass.: Harvard U.P.).

Mills, E. S. (1972), 'Markets and efficient resource allocation in urban areas', *Swedish Journal of Economics*, 74, 100–13.

Mirrlees, J. A. (1972), 'The optimum town', *Swedish Journal of Economics*, 74, 114–35:

Muth, R. F. (1969), *Cities and Housing* (Chicago: Chicago U.P.).

Muth, R. F. (1976), 'A vintage model with housing production' in G. J. Papageorgiou (ed.), *Mathematical Land Use Theory* (Lexington, Mass.: D. C. Heath).

Pines, D. (1976), 'Dynamic aspects of land use pattern in a growing city', in G. J. Papageorgiou (ed.), *Mathematical Land Use Theory* (Lexington, Mass.: D. C. Heath).

Rawls, J. (1971), *A Theory of Justice* (Cambridge, Mass.: Harvard U.P.).

Richardson, H. W. (1977), *The New Urban Economics and Alternatives* (London: Pion).

Richardson, H. W. (1978), *Regional and Urban Economics* (Harmondsworth: Penguin).

Riley, J. G. (1973), 'Gammaville: an optimum town', *Journal of Economic Theory*, 6, 471–82.

Schaeffer, K. H., and Sclar, E. (1975), *Access for All: Transportation and Urban Growth* (Harmondsworth: Penguin).

Solow, R. M. (1972), 'Congestion, density and the use of land in transportation', *Swedish Journal of Economics*, 74, 161–73.

Solow, R. M. (1973), 'Congestion costs and the use of land for streets', *Bell Journal of Economics and Management Science*, 4, 602–18.

Stern, N. H. (1973), 'Homogeneous utility functions and equality in "the optimum town"', *Swedish Journal of Economics*, 75, 204–7.

Thomson, J. M. (1969), *Motorways in London* (London: Duckworth).

Thomson, J. M. (1977), *Great Cities and their Traffic* (London: Gollancz).

Warner, S. B., Jr. (1962), *Streetcar Suburbs: The Progress of Growth in Boston 1870–1900* (Cambridge, Mass.: Harvard U.P.).

Weintraub, E. R. (1974), *General Equilibrium Theory* (London: Macmillan).

Whitehead, C. M. E. (1974), *The U.K. Housing Market: An Econometric Model* (Farnborough: Saxon House).

7 Beyond General Equilibrium

We have been critical of general equilibrium approaches to the urban system on two grounds – the problems of handling continuous variables simultaneously in both space and time dimensions, and the relevance of a dynamic path based on sequences of temporary equilibria. In this chapter we outline some operational alternatives to the general equilibrium approach and discuss their relevance to our primary aim of understanding and evaluating economic behaviour in a spatial economy.

The greatest advantage of assuming continuity in economic models is in the range of mathematical techniques then available for the derivation of solutions, particularly the differential and integral calculus. Without this convenient assumption it will usually be necessary to employ a mathematical programming approach. We shall consider two basic programming models which can be termed aggregate optimising and disaggregate sub-optimising approaches. In the final section of this chapter we shall return to the more familiar structure in an attempt to provide a link between these models and those discussed previously but omitting the assumption of equilibrium.

AGGREGATE OPTIMISING MODELS

The linear programming model has long been recognised to have particular advantages both in the representation of economic relationships and in providing an operational model for policy formulation. The class of models we shall discuss in this section is characterised by their assumption of a single overall objective function for the city. There are thus obvious links with the planning models of cities which follow in the Lowry tradition (1964) although based on much more precise and explicit economic relationships. Models developed from the basic Lowry formulation, such as those expounded by Wilson (1974) are complex in that they consider a multi-sector world and effective in that they can simulate land-use distributions but are none the less crude in their underlying assumptions. Essentially an iterative solution is adopted to balance the requirements of various employment sectors with residential use, demand and transport but based on a sort of planning-accounting system rather than on understanding of economic relationships and market activity. As such these models fall outside our sphere of interest, which is confined to economic behaviour.

The first attempt at a complete linear programming model did, however, emerge from a planning exercise. Herbert and Stevens (1960) produced an exceptionally detailed model structure of residential location using as an objective the maximisation of rent-paying ability subject to constraints on available land and population and ensuring the allocation of each household to a site. The model assumes the existence of different household types, residential types, and zones, each having a finite number. Households of type i budget a given amount, b_{ij}, to purchase residential accommodation of type j which in zone k would cost them c_{ijk} exclusive of site (rent) costs. If the area occupied by the choice is s_{ij} and zone k has a given area of residential land available, $\bar{s}_k$, then the problem can be written as the linear programme

$$\max Z = \sum_i \sum_j \sum_k n_{ijk}(b_{ij} - c_{ijk}) \tag{7.1}$$

subject to

$$\sum_i \sum_j s_{ij} n_{ijk} \leq \bar{s}_k \tag{7.2}$$

$$\sum_j \sum_k n_{ijk} = N_i \tag{7.3}$$

$$n_{ijk} \geq 0 \tag{7.4}$$

where n_{ijk} is the number of households of type i using housing of type j in k, and N_i is the total number of households of type i.

The objective (7.1) is based on the same premise as the bid-rent function which formed the basis of the residential sector in the continuous models of earlier chapters. The model has no explicit transport costs but for any given zone these can be incorporated into c_{ijk}. To obtain homogeneous preferences over the number of house types implies that the number of household types is fairly large. A difficulty is, however, that the amount of household type mixing within zones is limited by the linear programming property relating the number of non-zero-valued variables in the optimal solution to the number of constraints. Since there are K constraints defined by (7.2) and I constraints defined by (7.3) there can be only $K + I$ non-zero values of n_{ijk}. This suggests a fairly low level of social mixing within zones, which is a problem unless the zoning and household type classifications are exceptionally fine. Wilson has suggested that the use of an entropy-maximisation approach may produce a more satisfactory result here.

The problem with the Herbert–Stevens linear programming model is essentially one of its enormous data requirements coupled with a rather naïve allocational result. However, it should be pointed out that the model is intended as an overall optimising model rather than a simulation of an actual urban area. The variety of social mixes normally observed and the implicit 'cross-hauling' of the transport system are simply being shown as inefficient. This conflict between overall optimising on the one hand and the attempt to re-create or predict actual spatial organisations on the other is a problem which will dominate this chapter.

A much more complete linear programming model of the city is that suggested by Mills (1972). Mills' model starts with a grid pattern, with each grid square described by co-ordinates (i, j) relating its position to the city centre $(0, 0)$. The transport system is also based on this grid pattern such that the distance of (i, j) from the centre is $d_{ij} = |i| + |j|$. The city has production, residential and transport sectors, the overall objective being to minimise total operational costs of the city, production plus transport, subject to a wide range of constraints.

The production sector produces C commodities: $C - 1$ are goods of which a given amount $\bar{x}_c$ is produced for export, the Cth good is housing which is all consumed internally. Inputs are homogeneous factors, labour, L, land, A, and capital, K. Labour and capital are available nationally at fixed rates w and r per unit respectively. The wage actually paid in the city will exceed w by the locally determined cost of housing and commuting. Land is available at its agricultural rental value, r_a, per grid square. The boundary of the city is given by max $(|i|, |j|) = \bar{u}$. The technology of production is given by a range of activities determined by the capital–land ratio implicit in the height of buildings. The input-output coefficients a_{fcs} express the amount of factor, f, required per unit output of the cth good by the sth activity (the production of a unit of output in an s-storey building). The model allows inputs to be imported and assumes each worker requires one unit of housing.

The overall objective function is a complex expression of required production and transport costs. Each term involves two separate parts, one relating to the $4u$ suburban zones at each value of $i, j = u$ and one relating to the central zone where there is no transport of items necessary. The cost of production can be written as

$$Z_c = r \left[\sum_u \sum_c \sum_s 4u a_{Kcs}(u) + \sum_c \sum_s a_{Kcs} x_{cs}(0) \right]$$

$$+ r_a \left[\sum_u \sum_c \sum_s 4u a_{Acs} x_{cs}(u) + \sum_c \sum_s a_{Acs} x_{cs}(0) \right] \quad (7.5)$$

$$+ w \left[\sum_u \sum_c \sum_s 4u a_{Lcs} x_{cs}(u) + \sum_c \sum_s a_{Lcs} x_{cs}(0) \right]$$

the three bracketed terms representing capital, land and labour costs respectively.

The transport system has both capital and land requirements which determine its capacity. Assuming input-output coefficients b_K and b_A basic transport costs are given by

$$Z_T = r \left[b_K \sum_u 4u . T(u) + b_K T(0) \right]$$

$$+ r_a \left[b_A \sum_u 4u . T(u) + b_A T(0) \right] \quad (7.6)$$

In addition there is a congestion function which is approximated as a step function of the marginal cost q_m at a given congestion level m at which total traffic in the square is $T_m(u)$.

$$Z_M = \sum_u \sum_m 4u q_m T_m(u) + \sum_m q_m T_m(0) \quad (7.7)$$

The overall objective is then

minimise $$Z = Z_c + Z_T + Z_M \quad (7.8)$$

Various sets of constraints are necessary to complete the model. The production level of non-housing goods must at least satisfy the export requirements.

$$\sum_u \sum_s 4u x_{cs}(u) + \sum_s x_{cs}(0) \geq \bar{x}_c ; c = 1, \ldots C-1 \quad (7.9)$$

The total production of housing must satisfy total housing demands which are given by the total employment.

$$\sum_u \sum_s 4u x_{cs}(u) + \sum_s x_{cs}(0) \geq \sum_u \sum_c \sum_s 4u a_{Lcs} x_{cs}(u) + \sum_c \sum_s a_{Lcs} x_{cs}(0) \quad (7.10)$$

The remaining constraints relate to various aspects of the transport system. There are three types of transport flow internal to the city. It is assumed that all trade with areas outside the city involves a transaction at the city centre; thus all exported goods must be transported from their production square to the centre. Similarly all imported inputs must be transported from the centre to their production square. The third category is of workers commuting from their home square to their employment square. If $T_c(u)$, $(c = 1, \ldots C - 1)$ is the amount of x_c shipped through a square at distance u, $T_c(u)$ the number of commuters, and t_c $(c = 1 \ldots C)$ is the demand placed on the transport system by that shipment then total transport demand can be written as

$$T(u) = \sum_c t_c T_c(u) \qquad (7.11)$$

Further constraints ensure that the composition of traffic in each square at distance u is always the same for efficient usage of the total transport system; that workers always commute towards the centre for the same reasons and hence that residences are more suburbanised than production; and express the relationship between capacity and demand through the step function congestion effects.

A final necessary constraint is a land-use constraint ensuring that the total allocation of land to production, housing or transport in any square does not exceed its area.

The overall problem is of course quite large but not unmanageably so. Mills estimated that for a typical city of one million population occupying 250 square miles less than 2000 variables and 100 inequalities would be necessary to define it completely. The number of variables depends on the number of squares, number of goods and activities and the number of specified congestion levels. The number of inequalities depends on the numbers of squares, goods and congestion levels. Mills suggests a range of ten export goods, fifteen activities and five congestion levels and squares of one square mile.

Tests of this model yielded a number of results consistent with those established in the continuous models. Congestion was found to be quite consistent with an efficiently organised city, cost per unit carried per unit of distance being about five times as large at the centre as at the edge of the city and falling off fairly steeply. Similar results are found for the activity choice, represented here, it will be recalled, as the number of storeys in buildings, and hence the capital–land ratio or density. High concentrations of tall buildings are found in the centre with a rapid decline in density to a nearly constant level in outer areas where residential uses predominate. This pattern is repeated in the shadow prices of land identified from the solution to the dual model.

However, the model also produced rather disturbing features. Small changes in the assumed input-output coefficients, particularly a_k and in t_c led to extremes in land-use patterns – from a totally centred city with all production in the inner squares and all housing further out, to a totally dispersed city with employment equal to residence in each and every zone. Although this is unfortunate from the point of view of simulating city growth and development it does suggest two points of interest. Firstly, the development of concentrated cities could be largely the result of historical accident, particularly combinations of technology and transport resulting in concentration. Secondly, it suggests that planning the optimal city involves a very careful choice of both activities and transport parameters since there is potential instability. We therefore have to be extremely careful in rejecting such a model on the basis of its predictions without a great deal more careful examination.

The main changes in assumptions necessary to obtain greater realism would involve a considerable increase in the complexity of the model. Two major relaxations in restrictions have been examined by Hartwick and Hartwick (1974), firstly to allow the city's export-import trade to be conducted through suburban centres and not just the single city centre, and secondly to allow for intermediate goods which require internal shipment. This model required simplifications in certain other directions to enable numerical simulation but also made one good rather less dependent on transported inputs and outputs, producing a more suburbanised pattern. Other potential areas of development are to allow alternative transport modes, land-use controls such as zoning, plot ratios and similar measures, various fiscal measures of tax and subsidy, and alternative transport-pricing systems.

What then is our assessment of the aggregate programming model; how far does it help in our understanding of the basic problems of the spatial economy and in providing solutions to them? The first point is one that we have already noted: the use of a discrete, zonal, description of space is a positive advantage compared with the continuous distance functions of the models described earlier. The production sector has also been transformed from a single-commodity sector to a multi-product sector involving a range of goods produced by different activity techniques. However, this increase in realism is balanced by the need to assume linear production relationships and fixed production coefficients with no reference to the all-important agglomeration economies. The transport sector can accommodate the main features essential for a realistic model. The need to assume a step congestion function might be a little unrealistic in that congestion effects tend to emerge continuously; but on the other hand it is likely that a realistic pricing policy to incorporate congestion effects would operate discontinuously in this fashion.

The housing sector, which was noted as dominating the typical general equilibrium model, receives rather less detailed attention in this model. The rather troublesome relationship between households and workers has been noted before and this model offers no advance on this point. At least the linear programming model does allow explicitly for housing production, although it fails to account for the dynamic effects of sequential and non-reversible developments we have discussed previously. There is also no preference function over the housing characteristics, it being assumed that housing costs are described in such a way that simple minimisation is adequate.

This leads us to the major consideration, the significance of assuming an overall minimisation as an objective. The role of the model is seen as producing an optimal solution but one which it is assumed would arise from the operation of efficient markets. Mills identifies the transport sector as the key determinant here in that any non-optimal pricing in that sector will lead to inefficient allocations elsewhere. His model therefore works on the assumption that public-sector control of urban structure can be effected through transport pricing policy, the transport sector being in public control.

Mills' belief is that there is sufficient competition between developers and landowners to ensure that within the framework of these optimal transport prices resources are allocated within the city in the most efficient manner. This assumption may be questioned on empirical grounds, whether it is true that there is not significant monopolistic control of land even fairly close to the central area, where of course land is in shorter supply, or whether there is free competition between landowners and developers. However, there is a more serious problem which is largely independent of market structure and organisation, whether decision-makers within the urban economy do behave as the full optimisers the model assumes and hence whether the assumption of overall optimisation is an acceptable approximation.

There are two issues at stake here. Firstly we face the familiar question of what the objective function of the decision-maker is. The cost-minimisation objective is in effect the programming analogue of utility or profit maximisation in the more conventional model. Alternative theories have been widely suggested in the non-spatial literature. For firms, objectives such as sales or revenue maximisation or more complex hypotheses of so-called 'satisficing' behaviour have been examined and used fairly widely. For individuals, revisions of conventional utility approaches often simply involve the addition of further dimensions to the argument of the utility function, since this is much less precise than a profit function; but here too satisficing concepts have been suggested. The main effect of such modifications is to modify rather than overturn the predictions of the conventional approaches. One interesting application to an explicitly spatial model is that of Devletoglou (1971). The effect of satisficing is shown to be in terms of thresholds of behaviour rather than smooth transitions. Individuals therefore respond more slowly overall but in discrete jumps.

Such an idea is quite clearly relevant to many spatial situations. It would be nonsense to believe that individual agents, whether firms or households, responded along smooth transition curves from one situation to the next. Relocation involves substantial costs as we have seen, informational and monetary. Relocation may also be thwarted by the optimal site not being vacant and hence the move may have to wait until it is free, which may take a totally unpredictable time. But does this matter and do we require the model to predict precise individual behaviour patterns? We have argued earlier that this is not the objective. The primary role of the model is simply to understand average behaviour responses to particular situations and examine the conditions holding in equilibrium. As long as the behaviour of individuals is such that they compensate for errors so as to converge on the long-run equilibrium position divergences from the optimal path are not critically important. Such divergences may carry costs with them, costs which are not borne solely by the individual in question; but they are not fundamental.

Suppose, however, that such divergences are actually de-stabilising and having once occurred lead to a cumulative movement away from the optimal path. In such circumstances the model will require a more fundamental recasting since it will not involve just a temporary loss of benefits but a cumulative one which may require rather different corrective action. It is this second issue, the possible failure to attain or even approach long-run equilibrium which requires rather greater consideration in the following section.

DISAGGREGATE SUB-OPTIMISING MODELS

The class of models discussed in the previous section is characterised by two main features; they assume a convergence to a long-run equilibrium situation and a single aggregate objective function. The working of this model in practice thus depends crucially on the optimising behaviour of all agents in all sectors of the model, complete and perfect response to all market signals and perfect recognition of any departures from the optimum such that appropriate corrective action may be taken. Increasing interest has been shown by economists recently in the behaviour of economies when individual decision-makers are not perfect optimisers (Day, 1975). Most of this work has concentrated on the dynamic behaviour of individual sectors and typically without any consideration of spatial factors. It is clear from much of the argument of earlier chapters that for reasons of imperfect knowledge, search behaviour, uncertainty – all of which characterise space – this type of sub-optimising behaviour is likely to be typical of the spatial economy. The concept of sub-optimising behaviour by individuals implies disaggregation, since the degree of failure to optimise and the rate of adaptation of behaviour will differ at least between sectors and probably even between various classes of individual within sectors. It is how to allow for this adaptive style of behaviour and its effects on the overall performance of the economy to which we turn in this section.

The principles of this approach can be outlined very simply, although the translation of this into workable models involves considerable complexity much of which is beyond the scope of this book. We start with a single economic agent faced with taking a decision on the basis of a known set of information signals. The first decision to take is whether, on the basis of his objective function, he is in the best situation he could achieve with that set of information and his existing preferences and constraints. If he is not then he must take action in accordance with his preferences and constraints. However, he faces two problems: one is his lack of perfect information, such that what he perceives is not necessarily true and because of his ignorance and uncertainty he may have to search for information; secondly, he recognises that even if he can identify the adjustment to behaviour he must make to improve his situation he cannot always achieve that complete adjustment within any given decision period.

If our decision-taker is extremely myopic, to the extent that he assumes that certain information signals do not change as a result of his decisions, we have a situation reminiscent of early attempts to resolve models of oligopolistic markets. According to the nature of the assumptions made the market solution could be shown to be stable, as in the Cournot case where rivals' outputs are assumed constant, or unstable, as in the Edgeworth case where rivals' prices are assumed constant. In these cases we need to examine two features, whether a full optimising stable equilibrium will be approached and, if so, the speed at which the adjustment to this takes place. The critical factors will be the proportional adjustment to the assumed optimal position and the degree of error in that assumption. We are thus concerned rather less with the final equilibrium itself but more with the path to it and particularly therefore with individual agents' reaction functions.

A more realistic model would need to relax the assumed myopia of individuals and introduce strategic reactions of the type discussed with reference to game situations in Chapter 5. Here individuals are concerned not only with their own attempts to optimise but also with any similar reactions of conflicting parties to their own actions. A simple example will illustrate the complexities introduced here. A supermarket chain planning a location for a new store will recognise that other types of shop will be responding to the same stimuli (e.g. a new residential area or a new road system) and that this may generate additional benefits such that the precise site cannot be planned independently. It also realises that competitors will also respond in an attempt to secure new markets themselves. The entire calculation depends additionally on the assumptions made about the response of customers, existing and potential, to the new location.

In the absence of collusion all of these responses have to be assumed *ex ante* but the final solution will depend on how good those assumptions are. Once again we shall need to be concerned with whether the path converges ultimately to a stable equilibrium and the speed at which the adjustment takes place. In this case it is not sufficient simply to take assumed response parameters and examine the behaviour of the system, since non-myopic individuals concerned with improving their situation will also learn from revealed responses and accordingly many modify their responses in subsequent decision periods. Hence we also require a learning process within the model.

It will be clear even from this simple description that a representative model of this type will be unavoidably complex. Whilst it would be possible to proceed on the basis of continuous functions there is much to be said for retaining a programming approach. Many of the decisions which concern us are of a discrete nature and may often involve the sort of thresholds and discontinuities which are inconvenient in a continuous model. The use of discrete time-periods also has the advantage of enabling the use of varying degrees of myopia in adjustment. It is also important that we should stress the operation of the economy as a series of explicitly individual but interdependent decisions. The most useful approach to this type of problem is that of recursive programming. This differs from a dynamic programming model by not assuming that full optimisation takes place over the relevant time-period. A dynamic programming model seeks as a solution that set of decision variables which would achieve a given objective function over time, subject to the known constraints. The recursive format simply considers the relationship between given states and expected actions and attempts thereby to simulate a sequence of expected actions through time. This may or may not approach the full dynamic path according to the nature of the feedbacks. This contrast between recursive and dynamic programming has been characterised by Day (1973) as the difference between a positive and a normative approach; it attempts to reproduce what does happen as opposed to what should happen. The difference between the final states predicted by the two models could be a measure of relative inefficiency both in the working of markets and the ability of individuals to optimise.

The exact formulation of the model will, of course, depend on the nature of the specific problem to be solved and the outline presented here is only meant to convey the general structure. Like all programming formats the structure involves an objective function to be maximised subject to constraints. The maximand is a function of a series of decision vectors relating to the sequence of periods for which decisions are taken in the relevant period.

Thus we can write the optimal 'pay-off' for the time period t as

$$\pi^*(t) = \max \pi [X(t)] \qquad (7.12)$$

where
$$X(t) = [x^t(t), x^{t+1}(t), \ldots \ldots x^{t+\tau-1}(t)] \qquad (7.13)$$

the subvectors $x^{t+i}(t)$ referring to a known vector of decision variables related to period $(t+i)$ which are taken in period t. For the $(t+i)$th period in the planning sequence there exists a set of constraints,

$$F^{t+i}[x^t(t), x^{t+1}(t), \ldots \ldots x^{t+i}(t)] \leq C^{t+i}(t); \text{ for } i = 0 \ldots \ldots \tau-1$$

$$t = t_o \ldots \ldots \infty \quad (7.14)$$

where $x(t) \geq 0$.

The F^{t+i} are in the form of a vector of a known number of constraint functions, k_t, which may vary through time but is fixed in period t, and hence there are $k_t \times \tau$ constraints in all. Each constraint is a function of the $\tau \times m_t$ decision variables, where m_t is the number of decision variables to be determined for period t. This is a normal programming exercise for each period t and as τ increases it becomes a growing sequence of such problems. It therefore yields a solution in terms of an optimal decision vector,

$$X^*(t) = [x^{*t}(t), x^{*t+1}(t), \ldots \ldots x^{*t+\tau}(t)] \qquad (7.15)$$

where the vectors $x^{*t}(t)$, etc., are a sequence of planned decision variable levels for t, $t+1$, etc., taken in the period in brackets. We would not normally expect the *ex ante* planned level for $t+1$ in t, $x^{*t+1}(t)$, to be equal to the *ex post* planned level for $t+1$ taken in $t+1$, $x^{*t+1}(t+1)$. Moreover, the realised vectors, $\bar{x}^t(t)$, $\bar{x}^{t+1}(t+1)$, etc., would not be equal to each period's plans, $x^{*t}(t)$, $x^{*t+1}(t+1)$ either because of stochastic elements or changes in plan during a time-period. For each of the constraints F^{t+i} there exists a dual,

$$R^*(t) = [r^{*t}(t), \ldots \ldots r^{*t+\tau-1}(t)] \qquad (7.16)$$

in which each of the k_t components of each subvector gives the marginal expected pay-off from a relaxation of that constraint in the ensuing plan period.

The feature of the recursive programme is that a relationship is introduced between the parameters of the objective and the constraint functions. Let the parameters of the pay-off function be

$$\alpha(t) = [\alpha_1(t), \ldots \ldots \alpha_q(t)] \qquad (7.17)$$

and of each constraint function be

$$\beta^{ij}(t) = [\beta_1^{ij}(t), \ldots \ldots \beta_p^{ij}(t)] \qquad (7.18)$$

where $i = t \ldots \ldots t+\tau-1; j = 1 \ldots \ldots k_t$.

We can now rewrite the problem as,

$$\pi^*(t) = \max \pi[X(t); \alpha(t)] \qquad (7.19)$$

subject to,

$$F[X(t); B(t)] \leq c(t); x(t) \geq 0; t = t_o \ldots \ldots \infty \qquad (7.20)$$

where $B(t)$ is the matrix $B(t) = \begin{bmatrix} \beta^{t1}(t) \\ \cdot \\ \cdot \\ \cdot \\ \beta^{(t+\tau-1)k_t}(t) \end{bmatrix}$ \qquad (7.21)

The feedbacks are of three types:

1. $\alpha(t) = Z[x^*(t-1), r^*(t-1), \ldots \ldots x^*(t-s), r^*(t-s), v(t)]$ (7.22)

i.e. a connection of the pay-off function to past decision variables and exogenous influences, $v(t)$.

2. $B(t) = B[x^*(t-1), r^*(t-1), \ldots \vdots \ldots x^*(t-s), r^*(t-s), v(t)]$ (7.23)

i.e. a connection of the constraint function to past decision variables and exogenous influences.

3. $c(t) = G[x^*(t-1), r^*(t-1), \ldots \ldots x^*(t-s), r^*(t-s), v(t)]$ (7.24)

i.e. a connection of the right-hand side of the constraints to past decision variables and exogenous influences.
Hence the problem becomes,

$$\pi^*(t) = \max \pi \{ X(t); Z[x^*(t-1), r^*(t-1), \ldots \ldots$$
$$\ldots x^*(t-s), r^*(t-s), v(t)]\} \tag{7.25}$$

subject to

$$F\{X(t); B[x^*(t-1), r^*(t-1), \ldots \ldots x^*(t-s), r^*(t-s), v(t)]\}$$
$$\leq G[x^*(t-1), r^*(t-1), \ldots \ldots x^*(t-s), r^*(t-s), v(t)]; x(t) \geq 0. \tag{7.26}$$

The interesting feature of this is that the *ex post* decision vectors, i.e. $x^{*t+1}(t+1)$, are not equal to the *ex ante* planned optimum for that period, $x^{*t+1}(t)$, but will influence future plans through the recursive structure and hence the sequence of plans is, in a dynamic context, not the optimal sequence. In this way, whilst not producing a set of optimal plans the structure can be very useful in identifying the critical feedbacks in the system, which may be more useful information for the purpose of improving information flows and market signals such that future actual behaviour accords more closely with planned or desired behaviour.

The typical recursive programming problem can be solved in the format presented above since it is essentially a partial one, the examination of the behaviour of a particular sector, albeit not necessarily in partial equilibrium. For many urban problems this may indeed be a satisfactory approach to understanding behaviour within specific sectors since individual decisions taken within those sectors are responses only to anonymous market signals, prices, scarcities, etc., rather than to the overt decisions of individuals in other sectors. The general solution of urban allocation and structure problems becomes more complex, however, since we need to link the sequences of decision processes of several sectors through the exogenous influences at each stage as well as in terms of the determination of the sequences of interrelated *ex ante–ex post* decisions.

The recursion between sectors can be thought of as occurring in two different ways. Individuals may respond directly to the decisions of those in other sectors through modifications to $\alpha(t)$. In this case we need to specify carefully the exogenous influences, $v(t)$, which could actually relate to the decision variables $x^*_j(t-i)$, $i = 1 \ldots s$; $j = 1 \ldots n$, where n is the number of sectors. Secondly they may respond indirectly through market signal effects. In this case we need to consider such market interactions and the effects on market price under various assumptions concerning market clearing. This effect particularly affects the matrix $B(t)$ relating to the constraint functions since this is typically where market prices impinge. From the point of view of the individual sector this is equivalent to introducing specifically variables of the type $x^*_j(t-i)$, $i = 1 \ldots s$; $j = 1 \ldots n$ into the determination of $B(t)$. However, for the determination of an overall solution we need to know more about the working of the respective markets.

There are two possible assumptions, that the markets move into equilibrium at the end of each period, for example by constraining the markets always to clear period by period so that a sequence of temporary equilibria is formed, or that disequilibrium can exist. An assumption of equilibrium appears very unrealistic and almost contrary to the logic of an adaptive model which depends on the independent reactions of different individuals in the market albeit linked in a recursive manner, although it does have a number of convenient simplifying properties. It also raises the question of whether individuals attempt to move into full equilibrium: if experience gives them information about the way to modify their behaviour it should also convey information about the degree of success of such modification, and hence a policy of sub-optimising may be less costly than an attempt at complete optimisation in that period. The sets of reaction functions therefore incorporate information about this learning process in a fully disequilibrium sense where it is not just a market failure but a conscious decision of individuals within the market which causes the failure to achieve equilibrium.

It will be apparent that this approach enables a considerable degree of flexibility in the structure and design of a model of the urban system. At this level of generality it is not possible to draw even qualitative conclusions about whether the results will differ substantially from those of an equilibrium model. It does, however, seem reasonable to expect that, freed from a constraint to obey either a dynamic equilibrium path or even a period-by-period establishment of equilibrium, the urban economy may well exhibit a rather different structure. The next step is therefore to use simple versions of this model to simulate the development and structure of urban areas under, for example, different reaction structures. Such an approach may have an empirical base in the examination of the performance and structure of urban economies under different planning regimes such as would be revealed in a cross-national study. A further question is the extent to which such a model has implications for the evaluation of urban changes, most evaluation procedures having a basis in equilibrium values. An initial approach to this problem has been attempted in a recent paper by the author (Vickerman, 1979).

MODELS OF CUMULATIVE DISEQUILIBRIUM

Our primary concern is with ways of representing and understanding economic behaviour in a spatial world. To this end we have seen the relevance of relaxing the constraint or moving the individual into an equilibrium situation period by period. However, the complexity of the model has only enabled us to consider its basic form and not its consequences. In this section we shall examine some of the possible consequences of equilibrium for the economy as a whole and hence for the overall evaluation of change. To do this more conveniently we shall return to an aggregate model and one which typically ignores detailed spatial arrangements.

Writers on regional problems have for long been aware that the behaviour of regional aggregates such as income and employment does not accord with the postulates of an equilibrium theory. Full equilibrium in a multi-sectoral multi-regional world would imply the movement of resources towards high-productivity, high-income sectors and regions until falling marginal products in receiver sectors and regions balanced out rising marginal products in loser sectors and regions (Borts, 1960). As long as free movement of resources can occur imbalances will be corrected. This world, typical of much regional economics, does of course ignore space as an explicit phenomenon. It does not, however, require a great deal of manipulation to modify such a model to include a spatial element in terms of transport costs or other movement costs such that imbalances in marginal productivity and incomes can exist in equilibrium as long as offset by these spatial costs.

Empirical evidence, however, largely contradicts even such modified postulates. The regional problem in most countries is characterised by a cumulative divergence of the main aggregates, as are other spatial relationships such as the urban-rural imbalance found particularly in poorer countries and increasingly the relative inner-city poverty occurring in richer countries.

Whilst the evidence points to a failure for spatially differentiated economies to converge in the relative experiences of the different areas considered, the theoretical support for this observation has been lacking. Growth has typically been appraised in two-regional extensions of the basic neoclassical or Harrod-Domar approaches. These have been applied with a 'regional' bias to simple economies with two differing regions of the classic north-south type where, according to the origins of the model, one region has high productivity and high income and the other correspondingly lower values (Hartman and Seckler, 1967). Attempts have also been made to apply these to the 'urban' case using city-hinterland type models of which the urban-base theory is a special case (Friedman, 1973).

These models have been discussed in sufficient detail elsewhere not to warrant a detailed description here. Like all equilibrium models the attainment of equilibrium depends critically on the values of certain parameters. In the neoclassical model attention is focused on the growth of factor supplies, capital, labour and technical progress. In any one region the growth of capital and labour supplies depends both on internal forces, such as savings (for a given capital–output ratio) and the natural growth of the workforce, and on inter-regional flows responding to factor price differentials. Technical progress presents a more difficult problem – often it is assumed to be invariant over regions in order to separate it out from changes in the capital–output ratio due to other factors. It is the capital–output ratio which assumes the critical role in this model, since it is typically only by careful adjustment to this that the growth rate can diverge from that set by the growth of total factor supplies, particularly that of capital.

The Harrod-Domar model concentrates on the behaviour of aggregate demand as a determinant of growth in the Keynesian tradition. Again the critical variables are related to savings and the capital coefficient but typically in marginal form as the marginal propensity to save and the incremental capital–output ratio. The savings leakage in a multi-regional system is adjusted by the net balance of payments (as a proportion of regional income). Whereas the neoclassical model concentrates on ensuring that the equilibrium or optimal growth rate, usually called the 'warranted' growth rate, coincides with the 'natural' growth rate as determined by the rate of growth of factor supplies, the Harrod-Domar model, in the Keynesian tradition, examines the relationship between the 'warranted' rate and the actual rate. For equilibrium and convergent growth any discrepancies in the critical savings propensity or capital–output ratio must be balanced by appropriate trade to ensure stability.

Whilst it is always possible to obtain stable, equilibrium growth paths for a multi-regional economy which displays convergence from either of these model types, this result does depend critically on adjustment of parameter values. In certain circumstances it is possible to build in corrective mechanisms which ensure that such adjustment does happen, particularly under the assumptions of a completely neoclassical world. The problem which Harrod originally noted and which has formed the basis of most growth models in the Keynesian tradition, usually called 'Cambridge' models, is that without perfect knowledge and expectations the model is unstable in aggregate form. The actual and warranted growth rates may thus diverge in the aggregate and hence the rationale for convergence disappears. Much of the argument has centred on the problems which arise when the world consists of different 'classes' of economic agent, such as workers and capitalists, who respond in differing ways to the same stimulus, for example by having different savings rates at the margin.

Although the formal analysis of this problem takes us far beyond the scope of this chapter it can already be seen to be highly relevant for many of the problems we have raised so far. One of the earliest attempts to develop the disequilibrium model was by Myrdal, who used the concept of 'cumulative causation' (1957), although Holland (1976) has recently suggested that these ideas can be traced back to Marx.

Marx identified the imbalance as concerning the urban poor and their situation in many nineteenth-century English cities. Marx probably had, as Holland suggests, a better grasp of genuine spatial economic relationships than many later writers in the neoclassical tradition. He certainly did not envisage a self-equilibrating process by which urban areas absorbed surplus labour from rural areas until a nice balance of marginal products was achieved. The process was much more one which depended on capitalist concentration, the advantages accruing to large units of production and the external economies of agglomeration, sucking in increasingly specialised labour. The extent of that specialisation and of growth depended crucially on the quality of communications.

But what is substantially different in Marx's analysis is that the labour flow is not necessarily just a response to higher wages – there is also a strong push element associated with the mechanisation of agriculture and other clearances of surplus population from rural areas. Furthermore, Marx was explicitly concerned with labour market imbalance in the urban sector, the industrial reserve army, and the failure of the industrial urban sector to guarantee long-term employment for its workers as techniques of production changed. In addition to this Marx can be used to provide an alternative view of many of the intra-urban processes which we have considered, particularly his views on rent (Harvey, 1973). Here again it is the introduction of groups acting out of 'class interest' rather than the individualistic, egalitarian responses of the neoclassical model which produces the divergent and non-equilibrating results.

Myrdal's concern was to investigate why, whatever the initial stimulus to growth in a particular area, the expected processes of diffusion and neoclassical balancing via the productivity-price mechanism did not restore a balanced and convergent growth pattern for a multi-region economy. His primary contribution was to suggest that in addition to the 'spread' effects of faster economic growth in a particular area there were also 'backwash' effects which could negate that advantage. Spread effects imply that faster economic growth in a particular area generates beneficial effects in surrounding areas. Increased production at lower cost creates export surpluses which raise the standard of living for other areas whilst the demand for imported factors and materials raises incomes in these peripheral regions. However, the backwash occurs because of the absorption of factors, particularly essential risk capital and qualified labour, into the 'centre' region where they achieve higher rewards. This process reduces the possibility of the peripheral regions benefiting fully from the spread effects whilst the potential of the centre region is enhanced.

Myrdal's analysis is a useful characterisation of the way in which regions, just as nations as a whole, can get locked into cumulative upward or downward spirals. It does, however, raise the interesting question of the correct policy response to such a situation. Is it the duty of policy to attempt to break this circle in the interests of regional balance or to support it on the grounds that total national output and income will grow faster by concentration in the most suitable areas? The imbalances can, therefore, be compensated and still leave everyone at least as well off as previously. In the context of developing countries Hirschman, for example, has argued strongly in favour of maintaining imbalance between sectors as a stimulus to further growth. In the regional context, Perroux, writing at about the same time as Myrdal, identified a similar process in terms of the spatial polarisation of growth found in most developed economies (Perroux, 1955). The idea of promoting growth by harnessing this polarisation with specific attempts to implant such 'growth-poles' in backward regions has formed the core of regional policy in some European countries, notably France and Italy, for several years. Nevertheless it remains true that imbalances will occur and can lead to tremendous economic and social problems in both gainer and loser areas. It is time for us to attempt to put a little more meat on to the skeleton of the analysis presented so far.

Complete formal analyses of the cumulative disequilibrium phenomenon are relatively few. One model is due to Baumol (1967), and later modified and enlarged by Oates, Howrey and Baumol (1971), and is concerned with the problem of cumulative urban decline and the ensuing fiscal problems of decaying large cities. The other is an attempt by Dixon and Thirlwall (1975) to formalise a rather imprecise statement of a Myrdal-type structure by Kaldor (1970). This model is less concerned with disequilibrium as such than with the conditions for equilibrium in an extended export-led growth model which has a cumulative effect built in.

Baumol's original model was primarily concerned with the overall macroeconomic problems of urban areas and bears a strong resemblance to some of Kaldor's explanations of slow growth in the British economy (1966). The model assumes two sectors which are differentiated by their relative labour productivity growth. One, which can be characterised as a service sector, s, has constant productivity and the other, b, has productivity growing at a constant rate, r. This division occurs against the background of a homogeneous labour market such that wages are the same in both sectors, the wage level being determined by productivity in the more dynamic sector.

Assuming that labour is the only input, output, Y, in time-period t, can be written,

$$Y_{st} = \alpha L_{st} \tag{7.27}$$

$$Y_{bt} = \beta L_{bt} e^{rt} \tag{7.28}$$

The wage level can then be written

$$W_t = W e^{rt} \tag{7.29}$$

where W is a constant reflecting a base point for wage levels. Unit costs,

C, in the two sectors can be written as

$$C_s = \frac{We^{rt}L_{st}}{\alpha L_{st}} = \alpha^{-1}We^{rt} \qquad (7.30)$$

$$C_b = \frac{We^{rt}L_{bt}}{\beta L_{bt}e^{rt}} = \beta^{-1}W \qquad (7.31)$$

and hence relative costs are

$$\frac{C_s}{C_b} = \frac{\beta e^{rt}}{\alpha} \qquad (7.32)$$

i.e. increasing at a constant rate over time.

If prices are proportional to costs and demand for each sector's output displays unitary elasticity then we can write relative expenditure on the sectors as a constant, A, since

$$\frac{C_sY_s}{C_bY_b} = \frac{We^{rt}L_{st}}{We^{rt}L_{bt}} = A \qquad (7.33)$$

and therefore

$$\frac{Y_s}{Y_b} = \frac{A.C_b}{C_s} = \frac{\alpha A}{\beta e^{rt}} \qquad (7.34)$$

Equation (7.34) shows that relative output of the 'service' sector decreases over time.

However, if relative outputs do not respond in this way, either because output in the increasing relative cost sector is subsidised such that prices are no longer proportional to unit costs or because demand is price-inelastic or income-elastic, relative expenditures are not constant. From equation (7.34)

$$\frac{\beta Y_s}{\alpha Y_b} = \frac{L_s}{L_b e^{rt}} = K \qquad (7.35)$$

and if $L = L_s + L_b$

$$L_s = (L - L_s)Ke^{rt} \qquad (7.36)$$

$$\therefore L_s = \frac{LKe^{rt}}{1 + Ke^{rt}} \qquad (7.37)$$

$$\text{and } L_b = \frac{L}{1 + Ke^{rt}} \qquad (7.38)$$

so as t increases L_s approaches L and L_b approaches zero. Thus if output does not respond to relative efficiency the economy must increasingly transfer resources to the relatively inefficient sector and the rate of growth of output, $r/(1 + Ke^{rt})$, declines.

Baumol uses this simple analysis to demonstrate that there is no reason why the process of increasing costs and increasing shifts of resources into the increasing cost sector should cease by a self-correcting mechanism. Whether this analysis is, or is not, an accurate representation of what is actually happening in cities or regions is, of course, open to criticism: the important point is that the analysis demonstrates the logical possibility of cumulative decline which is not present in the self-balancing equilibrium model.

The later model (Oates *et al.* 1971) looks explicitly at the decline mechanism by introducing a recursive linking between output or income, Y, and a measure of urban deterioration, D. Each is assumed to be a linear declining function of the other so that

$$Y_{t+1} = r - sD_t, \ s > 0 \tag{7.39}$$

$$D_t = u - vY_t, \ v > 0 \tag{7.40}$$

From these basic relationships we get

$$Y_{t+1} = r - su + svY_t \tag{7.41}$$

which can be written as

$$Y_{t+1} = b + aY_t \tag{7.42}$$

Equilibrium for Y, Y_e, is that level at which $Y_t = Y_{t+1}$, i.e.

$$Y_e = \frac{b}{1-a} = \frac{r-su}{1-sv} \tag{7.43}$$

Since s and v are both positive so is $a(= sv)$ and if $a < 1$, Y_t will converge on Y_e, rising if $Y_e > Y_o$, where Y_o is an arbitrary starting date, and falling if $Y_e < Y_o$. However, if $a > 1$ then a cumulative divergence from Y_e will occur, growth or decline depending on $Y_o > Y_e$ or $Y_o < Y_e$. The stability of the model thus depends entirely on the value of the parameter a, which in turn depends on the values of s and v.

These critical parameters can be seen as being influenced by policy variables, such as tax rates and levels of public expenditure, and hence the overall behaviour of the local economy can be seen to be either controlled by or induced by policy decisions. For example, a more precise model could be written as

$$Y_{t+1} = \alpha + \beta S_t \tag{7.44}$$

$$S_t = \gamma + \delta B_t + \eta E_t \tag{7.45}$$

$$B_t = \theta + \kappa Y_t \tag{7.46}$$

$$E_t = \mu + \xi Y_{t-1} \tag{7.47}$$

Equation (7.44) expresses income as a function of the level of urban services, S, which is itself a linear function of the tax base, B, and education levels, E (7.45). Both the tax base and education levels are related to income levels. Substitution of (7.46) and (7.47) into (7.45) and then into (7.44) gives

$$Y_{t+1} = \alpha + \beta\gamma + \beta\delta\theta + \beta\eta\mu + \beta\delta\kappa Y_t + \beta\eta\xi Y_{t-1} \tag{7.48}$$

which can be written as

$$Y_{t+1} = b' + a'_1 Y_t + a'_2 Y_{t-1} \tag{7.49}$$

from which we can derive the equilibrium value of income as

$$Y_e = \frac{b'}{1 - a'_1 - a'_2} = \frac{b'}{1 - a'} \tag{7.50}$$

The critical factor here is again the value of a' ($= a'_1 + a'_2$) which depends on the effect of urban public expenditure on income, B, on the response of public expenditure to changes in both tax base, β, and education levels, η (which may be seen as an indicator of the relative appreciation of the activities on which public expenditure is spent), and on the responses of both of these to changes in income, κ and ξ.

The model above is a simple representation but it is already clear that there is little which can be said on *a priori* grounds about the stability or convergence of the model. Only a very special set of parameters could ensure convergence. Oates, Howrey and Baumol experiment with a few plausible values to demonstrate both the vulnerability of cities to cumulative decline and the critical nature of policy intervention which can itself be severely de-stabilising.

The Baumol-inspired models just discussed produce disequilibrating forces by a simple recursive linking of income to such factors as the tax base and education, which themselves depend on income. The model of economic growth formalised by Dixon and Thirlwall (1975) aims to explain such recursive linkages rather more precisely. To do this an explicit relationship between output growth and productivity growth, known usually as the 'Verdoorn effect', is introduced.

The model is written entirely in terms of growth rates of variables. The rate of economic growth in an area at time t is related solely to the growth of its exports, x_t.

$$g_t = \gamma x_t \tag{7.51}$$

The growth of exports depends on three effects, the rates of change of 'domestic' and 'foreign' prices and the rate of change of 'world' income, each with appropriate elasticities

$$x_t = \eta p_{dt} + \delta p_{ft} + \varepsilon Y_t \tag{7.52}$$

On the assumption that domestic prices, or more strictly the domestic prices of exported goods, are determined by a known percentage mark-up on costs, the rate of change of these prices will be determined by changes in wage rates, w, average labour productivity, r, and the mark-up, m. Therefore,

$$p_{dt} = w_t - r_t + m_t \tag{7.53}$$

The final relationship is the Verdoorn effect, expressing productivity change as determined by an autonomous component r_a and the rate of growth,

$$r_t = r_a + \lambda g_t \tag{7.54}$$

where λ is the Verdoon coefficient.

Substituting equations (7.52), (7.53) and (7.54) into (7.51) we can derive an expression for the equilibrium growth rate g_e in terms of the various exogenous growth rates and parameters,

$$g_e = \frac{\gamma[\eta(w - r_a + m) + \varepsilon y + \delta p_f]}{1 + \gamma\eta\lambda} \tag{7.55}$$

To interpret equation (7.55) we must recall that η is an own price elasticity and therefore $\eta < 0$. Since γ and λ are both assumed positive, variations in λ will be expected to have a positive effect on growth. Areas with a large Verdoorn effect will thus display increasing growth rates.

However, this finding is not sufficient to demonstrate that regions will diverge in growth paths – that will depend on initial conditions and the relative sizes of the main determining parameters. Stability requires examination of the behaviour of the model under various lag structures. Under a one-period lag structure in equation (7.51), i.e. making exports in t a function of price and income changes in $t-1$ it can be shown that the time path of g is dependent on the value of $\gamma\eta\lambda$. We know that this value will be negative since $\eta < 0$ but the critical factor is whether $|\gamma\eta\lambda| \lessgtr 1$. Growth will only converge on the equilibrium if $|\gamma\eta\lambda| < 1$;

for values greater than 1 a cumulative divergence will occur. Dixon and Thirlwall have suggested that reasonable values of the parameters, $\gamma = 1$, $\eta < |2|$, $\lambda < 0.5$, make it most likely that the model is convergent.

Convergence here means that areas will tend to approach their own equilibrium growth rates. These rates for different areas could, however, diverge, quite consistently with the model, due to differing parameters, particularly differences in the elasticities η, δ and ε, in the autonomous element of productivity change and in the Verdoorn coefficient. This implies that once again we have to face a world in which different groups of people respond differently to the given stimuli – even if the individual groups of people can adjust to equilibrium the differences between groups can be increasingly divergent.

BEYOND GENERAL EQUILIBRIUM – A SUMMARY

This chapter has ranged widely across a broad spectrum of models without coming to any precise conclusions. To a large extent this is to be expected, since it illustrates clearly the important role of constraining the possible range of outcomes which equilibrium plays in models of economic behaviour. Without equilibrium models tend to become imprecise and boundless. It is therefore appropriate to try and draw out some general themes before turning in the next chapter to the wider implications.

It will have become clear during the course of this chapter that the idea of equilibrium, particularly in a spatially differentiated economy, can mean different things. This is most clearly seen in the previous section, where we are concerned with, on the one hand, equilibrium paths for one region or town and on the other with the convergence or divergence of the paths of different regions or towns. To the extent that our interest here concerns the relative paths of the different areas we need to know whether a failure to converge is attributable to adjustment problems within the economies causing them to diverge from equilibrium or to a more fundamental instability in the system which leads to a divergence of equilibrium paths.

The problem is that it is virtually impossible to produce precise answers on *a priori* grounds. The conditions for equilibrium tend to depend on parameter values, those for convergence on both parameter values and initial values of key variables in the system. The answer is then an empirical one and thus should be fairly easy to determine. The parameters in question in the various models we have considered are of two main sorts, which we could term technological and response coefficients. The former are those which describe the technology of the economy in terms of input-output coefficients relating to the factor or transport requirements of particular commodities or activities. We saw how critical these were in the Mills model and they would also be in a precise statement of the recursive programming model. They are implicit rather than explicit in the non-spatial models of Baumol or Dixon and Thirlwall but would none the less be significant in a more detailed and disaggregate presentation of these models.

Response coefficients are those which relate economic behaviour to economic stimuli such as market signals. The importance of these is particularly seen in the Baumol and Dixon and Thirlwall models since the behaviour of these models depends on such factors as price and income elasticities, the Verdoorn coefficient and so forth. The problem faced with such coefficients is that they may be extremely difficult to determine in practice. The performance of the models discussed could only be assessed by assumption of probable likely values for these parameters. Such assumed values are based on more than random selection or hunch, they relate to well-established economic relationships, but their precise evaluation is very difficult. To obtain estimates of such parameters empirically requires the making of initial assumptions about the behaviour of the economic system to be assessed such that the estimates can be interpreted from observed relationships; the assumption of adjustment to equilibrium is common. Typically we may also face an additional difficulty, to which we shall return in the following chapter – that empirical estimates of response parameters can only be made from observations of actual responses to previous changes. The use of such estimates implies both that the nature of the change is similar and that the response itself has not changed. Frequently, as we have seen, the sort of problems we are concerned with in spatial economies, transport investments or major urban renewal projects, involve changes which are both so large and so different from previous changes that previously-observed responses may be of very limited value.

One of the main difficulties with the use of response parameters of the type found in the Baumol or Dixon and Thirlwall models, and indeed in most economic models of market situations using continuous functions, is that they seek simple single-valued parameters to describe complex behavioural relationships. Whilst we have stated earlier that it is not our concern to produce models which replicate precise individual decision-making processes, it may often be desirable to look rather more closely at 'behaviour' than does the conventional economic model. A simple value such as a price elasticity hides so much information and may make such sweeping assumptions that it confuses more than illuminates.

It is on this point that the recursive programming approach, although complex and to some extent still in its infancy, offers considerable potential. As we have seen, the recursive model focuses attention explicitly on the response function, a relationship between current decisions and a range of previous decisions and other influences. The objective here is to attempt to unravel the various strands of influences which combine to make the overall response reflected in an observed price elasticity or similar variable. It does this without needing to constrain behaviour into an equilibrium framework. Much remains to be done to obtain operational models of this type, but recognition of the problems associated with the traditional approaches is a first step towards improving both our understanding of the way spatial economies work and the basis on which policy decisions are taken.

GUIDE TO FURTHER READING

Some knowledge of typical aggregate planning models is a useful contrast to this chapter as embodied in the work of Lowry (1964) and most ably summarised by Wilson (1974). The basic Herbert and Stevens (1960) land-allocation model is oversimplified but a useful starting-point to understanding the more comprehensive model of Mills (1972).

The initial challenge to these models comes from the critics of optimisation, much of which is due to the influence of Simon's views on 'satisficing' (1959), embodied in Devletoglou's work on thresholds of behaviour (1971). A valuable introduction to recent work on sub-optimisation is given by Day (1975). Operational models of this sort of behaviour have concentrated on the development of recursive programming, which is usefully summarised in Day and Cigno (1978). Some implications of such models for the evaluation of urban change are developed in Vickerman (1979).

A useful starting-point to the understanding of more aggregate disequilibrium models is the review of regional growth theories by Richardson (1973) and, from a rather different standpoint, Holland (1976). Holland also discusses Marxist approaches, which have been more fully developed in an urban context by, for example, Harvey (1973). Two parallel developments in macro-disequilibrium analysis were stimulated by Baumol (1967) and Kaldor (1970) and can be traced in the ensuing applications to urban decline by Oates *et al.* (1971) and potential divergences in export-led regional growth by Dixon and Thirlwall (1975).

REFERENCES

Baumol, W. J. (1967), 'Macroeconomics of unbalanced growth: the anatomy of urban crisis', *American Economic Review*, 47, 415–26.

Borts, G. H. (1960), 'The equalisation of returns and regional economic growth', *American Economic Review*, 50, 319–47.

Day, R. H. (1973), 'Recursive programming models: a brief introduction', in G. G. Judge and T. Takayama (eds.), *Studies in Economic Planning over Space and Time* (Amsterdam: North Holland).

Day, R. H. (1975), 'Adaptive processes and economic theory', in R. H. Day and T. Groves (eds.), *Adaptive Economic Models* (New York: Academic Press).

Day, R. H., and Cigno, A. (eds.) (1978), *Modelling Economic Change: the Recursive Programming Approach* (Amsterdam: North Holland).

Devletoglou, N. E. (1971), *Consumer Behaviour* (London: Harper & Row).

Dixon, R., and Thirlwall, A. P. (1975), 'A model of regional growth rate differences on Kaldorian lines', *Oxford Economic Papers*, 27, 201–14.

Friedman, J. (1973), *Urbanisation, Planning and National Development* (Beverly Hills, Cal.: Sage).

Hartman, L. M., and Seckler, D. (1967), 'Towards the application of dynamic growth theory to regions', *Journal of Regional Science*, 7, 167–73.

Hartwick, P. G., and Hartwick, J. M. (1974), 'Efficient resource allocation in a multi-nucleated city with intermediate goods', *Quarterly Journal of Economics*, 88, 340–52.

Harvey, D. (1973), *Social Justice and the City* (London: Edward Arnold).

Herbert, J. D., and Stevens, B. H. (1960), 'A model for the distribution of residential activities in urban areas', *Journal of Regional Science*, 2, 21–36.

Holland, S. (1976), *Capital Versus the Regions* (London: Macmillan).

Kaldor, N. (1966), *Causes of the Slow Rate of Growth of the United Kingdom* (Cambridge: Cambridge U.P.).

Kaldor, N. (1970), 'The case for regional policies', *Scottish Journal of Political Economy*, 17, 337–47.

Lowry, I. S. (1964), *A Model of Metropolis* (Santa Monica: RAND Corporation).

Mills, E. S. (1972), 'Markets and efficient resource allocation in urban areas', *Swedish Journal of Economics*, 74, 100–13.

Myrdal, G. (1957), *Economic Theory and Underdeveloped Regions* (London: Duckworth).

Oates, W. E., Howrey, E. P., and Baumol, W. J. (1971), 'The analysis of public policy in dynamic urban models', *Journal of Political Economy*, 79, 142–53.

Perroux, F. (1955), 'Note sur la notion de pôle de croissance', *Economie Appliquée*, 7, 307–20.

Richardson, H. W. (1973), *Regional Growth Theory* (London: Macmillan).

Simon, H. A. (1959), 'Theories of decision making in economics', *American Economic Review*, 49, 253–83.

Vickerman, R. W. (1979), 'The evaluation of urban change: equilibrium and adaptive approaches', *Urban Studies*, 16, 81–93.

Wilson, A. G. (1974), *Urban and Regional Models in Geography and Planning* (London: Wiley).

8 Analysis and Planning of the Spatial Economy

We have now outlined all the analytical tools necessary for consideration of the spatial economy. We have also, *en route*, encountered most of the problems which are likely to arise in the operation of such an economy. It is the task of this chapter to draw together these various analytical threads into a coherent framework and to consider ways in which by so improving our understanding of the working of a local economy we can improve its planning and our evaluation of policy measures.

It would be convenient if we could deduce a comprehensive set of precise and universally applicable models from all that has gone before. It should, however, be fairly clear by now that the search for optimality in models of spatial economies is probably as fruitless as that for optimality in the economies themselves. The complexities involved in the problem mean that for a model to be soluble it must be highly simplified. The simplifications usually adopted have been either to restrict the analysis to a single-choice situation in which the interactions between both the various decisions of a single decision-maker and different decision-makers are ignored or to impose a highly restrictive framework of interaction as in general equilibrium models. The restrictions in the general equilibrium model arise both out of the simplicity of the decisions which can be considered and out of the equilibrium assumption itself.

The way forward out of this apparent impasse of models being either too restrictive or too simple derives from the discussions of Chapter 7. Instead of starting with the rigid framework of equilibrium we need to build up our picture of the spatial economy by a detailed consideration of the interactions and linkages between decisions and decision-makers. Crucial to this, however, is the recognition that optimal spatial planning is not a practical proposition in operational terms, although of course optimal equilibrium concepts may play a role as an ultimate target. Operational planning needs to concern itself with two basic questions – what is the best way of achieving a given goal; and what are the precise effects on a range of indicators of certain policy measures? The indicators and goals may, of course, be both spatial and non-spatial. In the latter category would be the basic macroeconomic variables, income, employment, investment and so forth. In the former category would be both spatial distributions of these and the purer spatial factors such as the welfare evaluations of changing accessibility and environment.

The discussion in the remainder of the chapter is most conveniently in four parts. Initially we shall outline some basic principles for spatial economic analysis and planning. In the remaining three sections we shall take the broad areas of transport, location and land use, and activity models for rather more detailed analysis. The primary concerns throughout will be of both practicality and relevance to policy, the role of spatial models in problem-solving.

PRINCIPLES OF SPATIAL ECONOMIC MODELS

The major problem in any spatial model is the mechanism by which space is introduced: how is it perceived by the decision-maker, how is it measured, how is it evaluated? The way the economist copes with these problems for most factors is to attempt to introduce some form of market in which it is traded to provide a consistent basis for answering these various questions. We have seen in Chapter 3 how this approach has been widely used in both transport models and location models. In the transport case space has typically been measured by the time taken to overcome it, and hence the concentration on both the measurement of how time is perceived and how it appears to be traded against other, more easily measured and valued, activities. In the location case the market for land provides an assessment of spatial benefits and hence the concentration on rent functions in so much of urban economics.

This approach does tend to avoid some of the critical issues in the precise definition and role of spatial effects since it reduces the spatial dimension to more familiar terms. There remains an ambiguity, therefore, in whether the spatial dimension should be represented as a characteristic from which individual consumers or producers derive utility or should enter on the constraint side as part of the resource cost of undertaking a particular consumption or production activity. The approach adopted here is that the individual economic agents do not derive any welfare directly from a spatial factor. Hence a particular location or unit of transport can be completely described by a set of characteristics from which the welfare is derived. The location or journey is a means of producing that flow of welfare-generating characteristics at a known resource cost. Decisions concerning spatial questions are thus non-separable from decisions concerning the relevant primary activity since they concern aspects of its production: any model must reflect this integration of different levels of decision-making.

There is a variety of ways in which this integration of decisions in spatial economic models can be achieved. Complete description of the decisions to be made will normally require a system of equations to be solved either simultaneously or recursively. Simultaneous resolution of the set of decisions will often be infeasible due to the number of possible choices for each level of decision-making. For this reason, and also because in many circumstances it may actually reproduce decision-making processes more accurately, a recursive solution of a sequentially ordered set of decisions is to be preferred. The method of linking the equations by calculating an 'inclusive price' at each stage which is then incorporated in the next stage as an estimate of the range of choices relevant to that decision leads to our characterisation of the spatial dimension as a price.

We could logically consider a single reduced-form equation for activity choices in which all spatial considerations were reduced to a single spatial price factor. In such a case space as a separate factor can be forgotten, since all spatial considerations are included in the current generalised prices of activities and choice could proceed as for any simple non-spatial model of behaviour. Here there would be a typical single-objective (utility) function maximised subject to a budget constraint in which the 'prices' and 'resources' had been generalised in accordance with observed preferences for the various elements in the choices – time, cost, comfort, convenience, attraction, etc. This yields a single implicit demand relationship for each activity in terms of the various prices and the overall resource constraint. The effects of a change in a spatial variable are traced by examining its effect first on the inclusive price, then on the activity pattern and then back on the various spatial demands for travel and transport modes implicit in or derived from that pattern.

This approach does have some rather troublesome inherent problems. First of all we have subsumed any preferences individuals may have over spatial factors under the single inclusive price on the basis of cross-sectional observations: if these preferences change then so do the weights attached to each factor, and so does the inclusive price. This is a worry in all cross-section-based results but needs additional emphasis when one part of the model becomes hidden in this way. Secondly, we have assumed that any constraints on behaviour are adequately reflected in the inclusive prices in such a way that the decision-maker is able to trade freely any of the generalised resources once they have been valued. Whilst it is true that individuals may trade activity characteristics in this way – for example consumers trade time for money by substituting a cheaper activity at a greater travelling distance for an expensive one close to home, and producers may trade location and transport costs against other inputs – there will typically be severe constraints on their ability to do so. We met this problem initially in Chapter 2 over the need for a time consumption constraint in the Becker model. This worry over the importance of constraints acting between spatial and activity characteristics would appear to limit severely the possibility for practical simplification of the model along the lines suggested so far.

Two alternative procedures remain, a simultaneous equation solution in which the constraints remain explicitly in the model and a programming solution which handles the relationship between the objective function and various constraints rather differently.

The simultaneous equation approach envisaged would still use the recursive method of estimating inclusive prices for part of the model but would resist carrying this through to the logical conclusion of the single-equation model. The various stages of transport choice could logically be combined since they deal with the same attributes for which constraints on substitution would not be necessary. It may, further, be possible to combine all the spatial aspects into a single equation or set of equations to be solved simultaneously with that for activities. This model explicitly states the production relationship between each activity and its associated spatial features, distribution of activity sites, transport requirements. This enables us to consider the various inequality constraints of minimum levels of activity associated with a given spatial input or maximum spatial input associated with a given level of activity which may exist for both 'technical' and preference reasons. The final interaction is, however, handled simultaneously, the individual choosing optimal activity and spatial patterns as a joint decision.

The programming approach is very similar in basic structure, involving basic objectives linked by series of constraints. It does have the advantage that it can handle non-continuous relationships and therefore can produce thresholds and discontinuities in behaviour more easily.

We thus have alternative ways in which we can approach the inclusion of spatial factors into decision processes as part of our modelling of behaviour; but how widely should such modelling be cast? It was noted early in Chapter 2 that the main way in which economists simplify their modelling of behaviour is to assume separability of decisions. In effect the utility function, or its corresponding dual-expenditure function, is thought of more as a tree in which decisions only affect those others which they depend on directly or which are directly dependent on them. Decisions on other branches of the tree are independent. The concern was raised in Chapter 2 that trading through the common medium of space may inhibit the achieving of adequate independence of decisions. It should be obvious that we cannot, for example, assume a separable transport expenditure function. The transport production of an individual is not independent of his activity pattern. However, can we legitimately consider a branching activity tree, each activity-branch of which has its own transport expenditure, and implicitly consider that there can be no substitution between the transport inputs to separate activities?

This then is the problem. Although goods may be completely separable as soon as we combine them into activities, especially activities with a spatial dimension, the separability is blurred. Individuals combine unlike activities to economise on spatial inputs – the incidence of multi-purpose trips, although only relatively recently identified in data and even less analysed, testifies to this. A high proportion of shopping is carried out on commuting journeys, a large amount of recreational activity is combined with journeys primarily for shopping, and, of course, the goods inputs for a wide range of activities are purchased on a single shopping trip. If we widen the analysis to consider families or households rather than just individuals the cross-substitution possibilities become even more complex.

Turning to location decisions very similar considerations come into play. Frequently studies of industrial location identify apparently irrational locations. This is easily explained in a static cross-section of existing locations by firms being out of equilibrium but not sufficiently so to cross the threshold which would make relocation viable. However, even within the smaller set of firms which are either mobile or potentially so (including those who have crossed the threshold mentioned above) irrational decisions are identified which are often put down to personal considerations of managers. If a wider range of activity decisions was accounted for, especially with explicit recognition of the realities of corporate decision-making under 'managerial capitalism', such decisions could appear less irrational – they are simply taken with respect to a wider range of activities.

A definitive answer to the range which needs to be considered is, however, probably not possible on *a priori* grounds. A rather more pragmatic empirical answer is called for requiring considerably more investigation of substitution possibilities and elasticities than has been carried out hitherto.

There is one further point of general principle which we need to address before turning to a more detailed examination of some practical problems. The techniques of recursive or simultaneous equation estimation enable us to cope reasonably well with the sort of interdependencies we are likely to face. The real question has been seen as one of defining the limits of interest of a particular problem as discussed above. However, our discussion so far has implicitly presumed that the various stages of decision-making are of the same order and in the same dimension. The utility and expenditure approaches are of this type. We identify an appropriate branch of various levels of decision each of which is taken with regard to an appropriate utility or expenditure function which is itself a sub-set of a higher-order function of the same type. In practice, however, spatial decisions are not about optimal levels of utility or expenditure on a continuous scale, they are about discrete levels of activity and more often about binary decisions, to do or not to do certain things. Even if we can determine for an individual decision-maker an optimal level of transport or locational expenditure, it remains a further task to turn this into an optimal decision strategy. A given level of expenditure could be translated into a number of different alternative transport patterns or locations.

This dichotomy between a continuous variable and discrete decision variables is likely to arise in pure spatial decisions concerning transport and location. A given level of shopping expenditure could be translated into certain shopping trips. Similarly a given level of potential investment expenditure for a firm could be translated into precise expansion plans which may involve relocation. The investment example does, of course, raise the possibility that not only spatial decisions involve this dichotomy. Individuals' activity patterns may also involve such a dichotomy. To a certain extent the problem is covered by technical constraints on the production function, whether of a household or firm: the time-consumption constraints met previously fall into this category. Such an inequality imposes minimum levels of the continuous variable which are required to effect an activity, but we must also remember that often individuals choose to operate under the inequality rather than the constraint, devoting more of one resource than is necessary because this changes the nature of the activity and makes it more desirable. Where, however, we run into serious difficulties is in the problems raised by externalities and the potential joint consumption arising between otherwise separate activities. This leads us back to the non-separability issue; but it is now not only the lack of clear demarcation between activities but also a lack of uniqueness in the translation of the aggregated expenditure into precise activity, and particularly spatial activity, patterns.

These then are the points of general principle, the *caveats* which must surround any attempt at analysis and policy prediction. The next stage is to be more positive and attempt to deduce what can be done rather than what should not.

THE DEMAND FOR TRAVEL AND TRANSPORT PLANNING

It has been clear from the start of our discussion of travel that a much wider concept than just the demand for specific transport modes is involved. Although we have concentrated on passenger transport most of the considerations apply with equal force to the consigning of freight. Travel demand models, as seen in Chapter 3, need to embrace choice of destination, frequency and timing as well as the simple choice of a mode. Moreover the further developments in later chapters have suggested that the effects may be more wide-reaching than this, involving activity patterns and ultimately locations.

Transport planning typically rests on the use of modal attributes as the policy variables, either through manipulation of money prices or a network improvement which concentrates mainly on a reduction in journey times. Whilst the policy variables may be reasonably clear the objective of policy is much less so. Sometimes it is simply a question of bottleneck removal concerning a single mode – minor road improvements, traffic control systems and similar moves. Increasingly concern has concentrated on policy to induce a change of mode in connection with what is deemed to be a more nearly ideal modal distribution of traffic. However, the definition of ideal is in practice difficult and the ability to induce a shift on the basis of the usual price and quality variables even more so. The concept of an ideal distribution between modes in practice is taken as a purely short-run definition concerned with an optimal distribution given the existing infrastructure, i.e. a level of traffic on each network consistent with the equalising of marginal social costs with willingness to pay. Whilst there is therefore a concern with marginal external costs, on the benefit side the private willingness to pay implicit in a demand curve is taken rather than a wider concept embracing the external social benefits associated with greater access and mobility, a concept involving recognition of complete activities rather than just travel.

An integrated view of transport implies more than just recognition that the overall effects of given change may differ from those implied by simple modal-split models when all the possible interactions are allowed for (Beesley, 1979). A fully integrated approach requires a redefinition of the social benefit of the travel so that we can both predict and evaluate the effects of a change. This means moving not just to the conventional second-best solution for the sector as a whole, allowing for the various cross-elasticities between modes as well as own price-elasticities when setting fares (Glaister and Lewis, 1978), but beyond the assumption that travel objectives are a simple minimisation of generalised cost. This also means moving beyond the view that transport constitutes a separable branch of expenditure which can be analysed independently of the sectors which it serves.

How can we realistically move forward to account for these considerations? Recent developments in the economics of consumer behaviour have tended to concentrate on the usefulness of the expenditure function rather than the utility function (Brown and Deaton, 1972; Gorman, 1976). These two are related through the duality theorem, since minimising an expenditure function subject to achieving a desired level of utility is equivalent to maximising a utility function subject to a budget constraint. Expenditure functions have the desirable property that the objective, the level of expenditure, is directly observable. A basic form of the model is to estimate budget shares as a function of total expenditure and prices

$$w_i = f(x, p_1 \ldots p_n) \tag{8.1}$$

where $w_i = p_i q_i / x$; $x = \sum_i p_i q_i$. The problem with expenditure functions has been the difficulty in defining acceptable, testable versions of equation (8.1) and the appropriate hypothesis tests (Deaton, 1978).

A particular problem for travel demand is that typical expenditure data are available for only broad categories of expenditure, such as transport, and appropriate subdivisions, such as expenditure on each mode. Such data prevent the linking of travel expenditures with expenditures on the associated primary activities. This leads us back to the separability problem of Chapter 2 once again and demonstrates the need for much more research on the links between expenditures which are interrelated in this way. This in turn requires some changes in the way expenditure data is collected.

A second strand of development which is valuable here is on the effects of household composition. This involves an explicit recognition that many decisions are not made by individuals acting alone but raises the question of how to aggregate the individuals within a household. Much of the effort here has gone into the definition of equivalence scales, particularly for non-working members of the household such as children (Prais and Houthakker, 1971; McClements, 1977).

We have, therefore, the essentials of theoretical developments which promise to offer a more satisfactory analysis of consumer behaviour. The essential next step is more detailed empirical research into the relative importance of the various linkages, the within-sector and the between-sector cross-elasticities with respect to variations in key elements of generalised price.

LOCATION AND LAND-USE PLANNING

In spite of its importance the modelling of location has reached nothing like the degree of sophistication of travel demand models. Consideration of optimal locations for firms or households raises such a variety of questions, as we have seen, that development into general equilibrium theories has seen the main thrust of research. Whilst considerable empirical work on location has been carried out this has not been at the same level as that on travel demand.

The planning objectives and policy variables are also rather different for location since a much greater use has been made of controls such as land-use planning procedures than of price (or other characteristics of generalised cost) inducements. The degree of behavioural understanding necessary in order to take planning decisions has therefore been much less. Objectives have, however, presented some problems. The development of fully optimising general equilibrium frameworks does have some relevance here since if fairly accurate control over land uses can be achieved it is important to have some concept of an optimal distribution towards which to aim.

The difficulty with this approach is the lack of evaluable objectives for the individual decision-takers, which makes it impossible to evaluate any losses or gains in welfare to individual groups as a result of the policy applied. Relatively little understanding of this issue on a local, urban, level has been achieved despite an increasing volume of studies on both intra-urban industrial location (Cameron and Johnson, 1969; Cameron, 1973) and the evaluation of residential benefits, particularly those associated with environmental improvement (Whitbread, 1978; Flowerdew and Rodriguez, 1978). Rather more work has been attempted at the broader regional level examining the effects and value of regional policies on industrial movement (Townroe, 1973; Moore and Rhodes, 1976; Ashcroft and Taylor, 1977). This is interesting since it is only at the regional level that any attempt is made to add price-related policies, such as investment grants and allowances and the regional employment premium, to the physical controls of Industrial Development Certificates. The evidence is far from conclusive, since while some redistributive effects of regional policy can be detected there is little evidence to suggest that regional policy can induce industrial mobility. Furthermore, the overall effects of such movement as does occur do not suggest that policy has been an enormous success (Moore and Rhodes, 1973; Sant, 1975; Buck and Atkins, 1976).

Once again the primary difficulty is the way in which the complex behavioural structure of decision-making can be represented. Some similar problems to the travel model are encountered but the solution is broadly the same in concept. For the firm we can consider the cost function, the production equivalent to an expenditure function, which a firm aims to minimise subject to output and other (technical) production function constraints. This cost function will vary with location. However, it does not necessarily mean that if a different location from the present location is identified as optimal the firm will relocate. First of all there will be financial and other costs leading to considerable inertia. Secondly, relocation implies new investment, in fact a large part of relocation involves the founding of branch plants in a new location. This suggests a three-stage decision process in which the first involves identifying the need for new investment, the second translates this into a potentially mobile plant and the third identifies an optimal location. These stages would be expected to be linked recursively so that the existence of a location could influence potential mobility and the investment demand of the firm. This view contrasts with the usual underlying assumption that the investment demand can be translated directly into movement potential without the constraints expected here.

Population migration is another problem which requires a similar approach. Models of inter-regional or other inter-area migration have relied very heavily on a basic gravity-model formulation of the type discussed in Chapter 3. The behaviour implicit in this model is simply that the population in an area reflects its 'push' or 'pull' to migrants as deflated by a distance deterrence. A more complete economic explanation needs to include reference to a wider range of economic variables but often these studies have tended to ignore the spatial element (Hart, 1970; Weedon, 1973). The closest attempt to relating migration to the operation of local labour markets in a spatial setting has been in the recent work of Gordon (1975, 1977), although this is still in an elementary form employing crude splits of aggregate flow data into streams with apparently different behaviour.

A more adequate theory of migrant behaviour at an individual decision level would involve similar considerations to the industrial relocation decision. Various stages of identifying non-optimality in the current location, identifying better locations and assessing the net gain from a move are involved. We can recognise that since a large part of migration also involves a change of employment rather different structures would obtain for employed and unemployed migrants and indeed for different types of labour market. That part of a migration flow which does not involve a change of job involves yet more different considerations. Even this simple look at the requirements of a migration model suggests that, just as with transport models, aggregate flows tell us nothing about migrant behaviour and may confuse many issues. Only by taking a much less aggregate look at, first of all, specific flows and then the behaviour of individual migrants and non-migrants can we hope to understand migration patterns and begin to evaluate them.

We can also note that it is migration decisions probably more than any other which require analysis at a household rather than an individual level. Migration typically involves all the members of a household and hence requires a readjustment of activity patterns by all such members: explicit recognition of this jointness is necessary for adequate modelling. The effects of varying family situations on achieved migration have been highlighted recently by Mincer (1978).

The main theme on location is that location decisions are constantly being made by any rational decision-maker. It is a mistake, therefore, for any model to concentrate solely on the movers. We need to know which locational characteristics enter the decision-maker's objective function but also how any potential relocation identified as desirable is translated into an actual move. For both firms and families much more research needs to be carried out on this linkage before optimal policies can be identified and evaluated.

ACTIVITIES AND SPATIAL ECONOMIC PLANNING

Whereas the discussions of travel and location have involved fairly specific consideration of the principal issues involved it is much more difficult to focus on such issues in the much more general area of the activities themselves. Many of the explicitly spatial issues of activity planning are of course covered by the more specific questions of travel and location. The planning of, for example, recreation, or schools, or libraries is principally concerned with issues of their location and the provision of access and the evaluation of these characteristics. Such planning implies that these activities feature in both potential consumers' decisions about location and travel patterns and suppliers' decisions about location and distribution. If this is so then we have no further points to consider. There are, however, two general issues which we have not taken up in this chapter which deserve consideration for completeness, the question of spatial competition and the more general question of the behaviour of economic aggregates.

The organisation of markets in the spatial economy has not featured very strongly in this book. Our concern has been primarily with those areas of public goods and externalities where policy intervention is more often seen as essential rather than just desirable. Undoubtedly, however, there are important issues here which should feature in any attempt at policy-making and planning. The main result of attempts to translate models of firms and industries into a spatial environment is that free entry does not reduce profits to normal. Spatial economies are built on the existence of increasing returns to scale and it is recognition of this which, as Kaldor (1972) has most forcefully stressed, renders the conventional models, not only of perfect competition but also of equilibrium itself, inappropriate. The spatial economy highlights, therefore, the perennial problem of economics: those features which bring the potential for gain into society (as increasing returns support the growth of urban areas and the increase in incomes and welfare ensuing) also introduce the potential for certain groups to obtain and wield economic power (as increasing returns lead to the growth of larger organisations with monopoly power).

There is, therefore, implicit in the existence of a spatial economy a conflict between growth and distribution; and it is this which dominates planning considerations concerning economic aggregates. The discrepancies in economic performance between regions of an otherwise unified economy have dominated (non-spatial) regional economics. Much of the work here has concentrated on either the likelihood of convergence in a free market situation or the effects of policies designed to eliminate discrepancies. We have seen in Chapter 7 how implausible theories of self-balance are, a view most forcefully expressed by Holland (1976). Holland's further contribution has been to relate market structure to this regional problem and in particular to examine the effects on regional structure and performance of large and multi-national companies. The economic power of such concerns is often so great as to thwart any attempt by a government to achieve a redistribution.

Increasingly concern has focused on more precise problems within this regional problem. It is really only at the sub-regional level that space has been incorporated into models or policy-making with any precision. The region is usually too large and heterogeneous an area for efficient policy-making – concentration on regional aggregates can hide often more pressing problems within. The attention given to inner cities is a current example of attempts to understand the inner workings of areas which have suffered cumulative decline with reference to a wide range of indices, multiple deprivation as it has come to be called. This is only a start, however. Already there is recognition of the continuing problems of rural areas, especially as far as accessibility and transport are concerned (Centre for East Anglian Studies, 1978). Beyond this the multiple problems of spatial relationships in the large metropolitan areas are likely to come to the fore, particularly the increasing problems of maintaining economic progress in very large conurbations in an era of high energy costs. Outer suburban commuter belts may not be traditionally populated by the most deprived groups, but their residents have borne a very large part of the transitional costs with increasing fuel prices over the last decade.

This movement away from the traditional regional economic policy to policies for selected areas carries with it the need for much more detailed understanding of the workings of spatial economies. To understand why cumulative decline sets in in inner urban areas, what the implications of zero public transport are on rural communities or what the effects of rising fares or fuel costs are on commuterland requires detailed analysis of all the interactions between sectors in the local economy. Some greater knowledge of this will lead us towards the possibility of a more integrated form of economic policy for the general welfare.

CONCLUDING REMARKS

There is no easy and precise conclusion we can set out for this book. It has been concerned with the development not so much of conclusive and directly testable models but more with a set of concepts and a system of thought. It is based on the belief that economics can have much to say about the organisation and working of society and that for an adequate view of that society we must incorporate the spatial dimension within which we all operate. There is no intrinsic difficulty in modifying basic microeconomics to introduce space; but having done so a number of challenging problems, and new insights, emerge.

The next stage is to move towards the development of more formal and testable models. It is to be expected that these may lack the elegance of the traditional models of economic equilibrium but they may thereby get closer to an explanation of how certain aspects of society work.

GUIDE TO FURTHER READING

Ideally this chapter should be read in conjunction with a text on the more practical aspects of planning. Wilson (1974) provides an interesting contrast in approach to the stance adopted here. Holland (1976) adopts an even less formalised and more polemical position. A valuable review of spatial planning theories and policies covering several countries is Hall (1974), and Thomson (1977) has reviewed transport conditions and policies in no fewer than thirty of the world's major cities. A very readable book which places it all in context is that of Schaeffer and Sclar (1975).

REFERENCES

Ashcroft, B., and Taylor, J. (1977), 'The movement of manufacturing industry and the effect of regional policy', *Oxford Economic Papers*, 29, 84–101.
Beesley, M. E. (1979), *The Influence of Measures Designed to Restrict the Use of Certain Transport Modes*, Round Table 42, Economic Research Centre, European Conference of Ministers of Transport, November, 1978 (Paris: OECD, 1979).
Brown, A., and Deaton, A. (1972), 'Models of consumer behaviour: a Survey', *Economic Journal*, 82, 1145–236.

Buck, T. W., and Atkins, M. H. (1976), 'The impact of British regional policies on employment growth', *Oxford Economic Papers*, 28, 118–32.

Cameron, G. C. (1973), 'Intra-urban location and the new plant', *Papers and Proceedings of the Regional Science Association*, 31, 125–43.

Cameron, G. C., and Johnson, K. M. (1969), 'Comprehensive urban renewal and industrial relocation – the Glasgow case', in S. C. Orr and J. B. Cullingworth (eds.), *Regional and Urban Studies* (London: Allen & Unwin).

Centre for East Anglian Studies (1978), *Rural Transport and Accessibility* (Norwich: University of East Anglia).

Deaton, A. (1978), 'Specification and testing in applied demand analysis', *Economic Journal*, 88, 524–36.

Flowerdew, A. D. J., and Rodriguez, F. (1978), *Effect of Renewal in Residents' Benefits and Welfare* (London: Centre for Environmental Studies).

Glaister, S., and Lewis, D. L. (1978), 'An integrated fares policy for transport in Greater London', *Journal of Public Economics*, 9, 341–55.

Gordon, I. R. (1975), 'Employment and housing streams in British inter-regional migration', *Scottish Journal of Political Economy*, 22, 161–77.

Gordon, I. R. (1977), 'Regional interdependence in the United Kingdom economy', in W. W. Leontief (ed.), *Structure, System and Economic Policy* (Cambridge: Cambridge U.P.).

Gorman, W. M. (1976), 'Tricks with utility functions', in M. Artis and A. R. Nobay (eds), *Essays in Economic Analysis* (Cambridge: Cambridge U.P.).

Hall, P. G. (1974), *Urban and Regional Planning* (Harmondsworth: Penguin).

Hart, R. A. (1970), 'A model of inter-regional migration in England and Wales', *Regional Studies*, 4, 279–96.

Holland, S. (1976), *Capital versus the Regions* (London: Macmillan).

Kaldor, N. (1972), 'The irrelevance of equilibrium economics', *Economic Journal*, 82, 1237–55.

McClements, L. D. (1977), 'Equivalence scales for children', *Journal of Public Economics*, 8, 191–210.

Mincer, J. (1978), 'Family migration decisions', *Journal of Political Economy*, 86, 749–73.

Moore, B., and Rhodes, J. (1973), 'Evaluating the effects of British

regional economic policy', *Economic Journal*, 83, 87–110.
Moore, B., and Rhodes, J. (1976), 'Regional economic policy and the movement of manufacturing firms to development areas', *Economica*, 43, 17–31.
Prais, S. J., and Houthakker, H. S. (1971), *The Analysis of Family Budgets*, 2nd ed. (Cambridge: Cambridge U.P.).
Sant, M. (1975), *Industrial Movement and Regional Development: the British Case* (Oxford: Pergamon Press).
Schaeffer, K. H., and Sclar, E. (1975), *Access for All: Transportation and Urban Growth* (Harmondsworth: Penguin).
Thomson, J. M. (1977), *Great Cities of the World* (London: Gollancz).
Townroe, P. M. (1973), 'The supply of mobile industry: a cross section analysis', *Regional and Urban Economics*, 2, 371–86.
Weedon, R. (1973), 'Interregional migration models and their application to Great Britain', in *N.I.E.S.R. Regional Papers II* (Cambridge: Cambridge U.P.).
Whitbread, M. (1978), 'Two experiments to evaluate quality of residential environments', *Urban Studies*, 15, 149–66.
Wilson, A. G. (1974), *Urban and Regional Models in Geography and Planning* (London: Wiley).

Author Index

181

Subject Index

184